Glad Tidings

With best wishes for a
Happy New Year!
Jennifer Flanders

—DECEMBER 2011—

Glad Tidings

The First Twenty-Five Years
of Flanders Family Christmas Letters

Jennifer Flanders

PRESCOTT PUBLISHING

Scripture references are taken from the authorized version KING JAMES HOLY BIBLE.

Photographs without credits are courtesy of the Flanders family.

GLAD TIDINGS: THE FIRST TWENTY-FIVE YEARS OF FLANDERS FAMILY CHRISTMAS LETTERS.

www.flandersfamily.info

http://prescottpublishing.org

ISBN: 978-0-9826269-8-6
LCCN: 2011943917

- Contents -

Introduction

One of my favorite parts of the holiday season is getting a bundle of Christmas cards delivered daily to my mailbox. I love the festive stamps, the bright red and green envelopes, the glittery greeting cards, and the family portraits. But I especially love the long, newsy letters we receive this time of year.

I know I'm dating myself to say it, but before the advent of Facebook, email, or the Internet, sending Christmas letters was the preferred method for keeping in touch with far off family and friends. These annual updates played a vital role in conveying news and marking important events.

In the beginning, this was my goal in writing the letters you now hold in your hand. My husband and I began our marriage with lots of friends and family scattered far and wide, yet little money for travel or long-distance phone calls. Our Christmas updates helped fill the gap. For the price of postage, we could send an annual summary of any recent changes in our lives, thereby doing our part to keep those relationships alive.

I'll be the first to admit that my earliest letters were a little dry. But as our family grew, my reasons for writing these letters changed. I found myself writing not so much to *inform*, but to *remember*. Although I continued to share what I'd written with our family and friends, I was really writing for myself. The letters allowed me to freeze those moments in time that I wished never to forget—significant milestones, everyday graces, hard-learned lessons, crazy mistakes, funny remarks. I wrote down the things that made me think or smile or laugh or cry, the things I wanted to treasure in my heart and to ponder for years to come.

It was a subtle shift, really, but it elicited an unexpected response. This willingness to share our foibles, to laugh at ourselves, to be sincerely vulnerable, allowed others to connect with us in a way that a brag sheet could never do. I guess it made our family more *real* and more accessible, because we began to get requests for extra copies of our updates.

Never mind that most of our letters were four pages long—people were passing them around the dinner table, forwarding them to friends, saving them in three-ring binders. I had one friend tell me that her husband insisted on reading the entire thing aloud at his office party one Christmas. We even received postcards from complete strangers, asking to be put on our mailing list.

It was really bizarre.

But it explains why, when I decided to publish our first twenty-five letters in a book to give our kids and grandkids, my husband urged me to make copies available to people outside our family, as well.

So here it is, for anyone who cares to read it. I hope you'll enjoy our little walk down memory lane. If so, drop us a line and let us know. We love getting mail!

With love and prayers,

Jennifer Flanders
November 27, 2011

1987

Okay, I admit it. We didn't actually *send* a Christmas update the first year we were married. We were too busy going to school, planning a wedding, and keeping house to think about recording any highlights from that moment in time for the sake of our posterity. But now, some twenty years later, we've compiled our recollections of those days so that our family history might be complete.

January of 1987 began as have so many years that followed—with a resolution to get more exercise. To that end, Doug and Jennifer both joined President's Health Club. It was really just an excuse to spend time together, since we were still pretending that we didn't *date*. Neither of us needed to lose weight: Doug was a rail at 6'3" and 160 lbs, and Jennifer had already shed the pounds she'd gained in college (they fell off as soon as she graduated and moved out of the dorms, away from the greasy meals served in the school cafeteria). It's just as well that weight loss *wasn't* the goal, as there was a Dunkin Donuts across the street from the health club, and we stopped in after every workout to split an assorted *dozen*. We'd sit in the parking lot feasting on apple fritters and chocolate éclairs while reading the works of Charles Spurgeon, debating the points of Calvinism, comparing our views on family planning, discussing the merits of homeschooling, and evaluating all the exciting possibilities that the future spread before us.

School was back in full swing by February. Doug was working on his bachelor's degree at Dallas Baptist and waiting tables at Café Acapulco. Jennifer was working on her master's at SMU and teaching business calculus labs. The separation seemed almost unbearable. Doug would sometimes skip his own classes to come sit in on Jennifer's, partly because he missed her, partly to stake his claim. When one young man under Jennifer's tutelage kept bringing her roses (in the vain hope that it would improve his grade), Doug told him in no uncertain terms that such behavior would not be tolerated. "She may not have a ring on her finger *yet*, but it's just a matter of time…."

The time came sooner than expected, when we went to Corpus Christi the following month to visit Doug's grandparents. As soon as we told them we were planning to marry, Nanny reached over and patted Jennifer on the knee. "Then we'd better get the rings sized," she enthused, slipping the wedding set off her own finger and dropping it at Taylor Brothers that very afternoon. It was ready on March 18th, and Doug formally proposed on bended knee in his grandparents' living room that evening. Nanny and Poppy served as witnesses (and provided what *coaching* they deemed necessary). Doug's grandmother, incidentally, was not ringless for long. She soon selected a replacement that looked just like the one she gave away, only her new diamond was bigger and was set in platinum.

Our excitement mounted in April when we were chosen as contestants for *The Nearly-Wed Game* at a bridal event hosted by Macy's Department Store. We were certain we'd win—after all, we knew *everything* about each other. Hadn't we spent the past twelve months baring our souls to one another? Unfortunately, the emcee eschewed philosophical inquiries in favor of frivolous ones, and we finished *dead last*. We were given a consolation prize to make up for our embarrassingly poor performance: two full sets of monogrammed bath towels (our color choice), plus a $50 gift certificate. The *first* place winners got a tiny clay pot for simmering potpourri.

One of Jennifer's professors summoned her to his office in May to chastise her for crocheting in class. She'd been doing needlework *for years* to improve her focus. All through high school, college, and graduate school, not a single teacher had ever called her on it. Now this instructor was commanding her to cease and desist, as he found the habit terribly distracting. Jennifer burst in to tears. "I won't be able to hear a word you say if I don't have *something* to keep my hands busy," she blubbered. "I'll be a million miles away—getting *married*!" Already, her head was full to bursting with cakes and dresses and flowers and invitations and a thousand other details jockeying for attention. That poor professor hadn't expected such an emotional response. He stammered an apology, told her not to cry, said he didn't realize she had "a *problem*", and agreed she could "keep on knitting," provided she sat in the back of the classroom to do it. So she did.

Doug and Jennifer had been attending EMT school at Baylor University Medical Center on the weekends (another ploy for spending time together). By June, we were both certified as Emergency Medical Technicians. Doug was already working full-time as an ER clerk at Baylor, but promptly took a second job driving an ambulance for the Mesquite Rodeo on the weekends. From his perch beside the starting box, he could lay one hand on the rump of a bull and another atop the television camera that broadcast the event. It was lots of fun—until a rider got gouged or stomped. Then it was terrifying.

Jennifer spent the summer working on her wedding dress. When time came for her mother's family reunion in July, she took scads of re-embroidered lace along with her to Oklahoma. Her aunts sat around the kitchen table all weekend and helped to bead it while they visited. Progress had been slow at home, since Jennifer didn't want Doug to see the dress before the wedding, but did want to spend every possible minute in his company. It took a second solitary week in Madill to get the dress ready for her bridal portraits. Even then, part of the lace was held on by straight pins; the front motif wasn't actually *sewn on* until a couple of hours before she wore it down the aisle.

At long last, Doug met Jennifer at the altar on August 15th. The setting was magnificent: First Baptist Church of Dallas with its stained glass, red carpet, tapered candles, fresh flowers, trailing ivy, and white satin ribbon. The music was incredible: organ, trumpet, violin, a contingent of forty voices from the Dallas Symphony Chorus. The ceremony was inspiring: taking vows, exchanging rings, sharing communion, lighting the unity candle. Yet none of these niceties guaranteed our marriage would *endure*. As we look back at our wedding pictures and video now, we are struck by how very *young* we were. What must our family and friends have been thinking as they watched the proceedings that evening? Did they wonder how long we would last? By God's grace and mercy, our marriage not only *survived*, it *thrived*, although we confess there have been a few rough spots along the way.

There has been only one Christmas— the rest are anniversaries.

W. J. Cameron

For starters, there was the honeymoon. Jennifer's father drove us to the airport, cutting across five lanes of traffic and jumping a median at 70 mph to get us there on time. He nearly missed his exit—and *we* nearly missed *the rest of our lives*. Transportation woes followed us to Florida. Our vacation package included a rental car, but neither of us was allowed to *drive* it. Doug had a valid license but wasn't old enough; Jennifer was old enough but had let her license expire (why renew on her birthday in April when she'd have to change it again after the wedding in August?) We ended up taking the hotel shuttle to Epcot and Disney World, then walking everywhere else (which meant, among other things, eating all our meals at a Denny's across the street). We set aside one day for an ocean voyage, only to discover that it was the *one* day the ship didn't run. It sailed 364 days a year, including Christmas, but on the third Wednesday of every August, it was dry-docked so that the barnacles could be scraped off its hull. (Is it any wonder that Jennifer would become so compulsive thereafter about making meticulous itineraries for our family vacations?)

After settling into our apartment and starting back to school in September, we found out Jennifer was *pregnant*. This may explain why the rest of 1987 still seems a little foggy.

Her morning sickness wasn't bad, but the fatigue was overpowering. From sun-up to sun-down, all she could think about was *sleep*. That fixation didn't set so well with Doug, whose mind was preoccupied with another consuming thought. Working two jobs and going to school full time didn't make a *dent* in his energy level!

By October, we were forced to face the facts: Dirty dishes *don't* wash themselves. We could have made short work of the stack in our sink had we tackled them right away, but after procrastinating for weeks on end, we had to deal with mold growing in the bottom of our milk glasses, a swarm of midges hovering over the mound, and a sour stench that permeated our entire kitchen. It was gross, but we learned our lesson: wash up immediately—or, better yet, *eat out*.

November took us back to Corpus Christi to spend Thanksgiving with Doug's grandparents. We had planned to spend Christmas with Jennifer's, but received word the following week that her Papa had passed away quite unexpectedly. It made us wish we'd alternated the other way around. We were shocked by the news and grieved to think that our children would not know their great-grandpa this side of heaven.

By December, Jennifer had almost finished writing the thank you notes for all our wedding gifts. *Almost*, but not quite. It would be another two months before she wrote the last

one, for an Anchor Hocking storage set which had no enclosure. We never mailed that final note, because we never found out who gave us the gift. Nor did we mail a holiday newsletters that first year, though we did send greeting cards to a handful of friends and family, which simply said: We hope you have a Merry Christmas.

Love,
Doug and Jennifer

1988

Why our apartment complex insisted we rent an extra 350 square feet to accommodate one tiny infant is more than I can understand—baby *still* sleeps in bed between us while the nursery stands empty—but rules are rules, so in January we transferred all our worldly goods from a cozy one-bedroom flat to a slightly-more-spacious two-bedroom studio. As we don't own much, this didn't take long. Doug was able to cart most of our stuff down the block on his back, including our sofa (a tufted vinyl settee that was missing three buttons), our bed (a queen-size mattress, no frame), and our kitchen table (a drop-leaf Duncan Phyfe with water marks and one wobbly leg).

He might have saved himself the trouble had we waited another month. Most of those second-hand furnishings were replaced with the *real thing* in February. We spotted a notice in the Sunday paper that a North Dallas furniture store was going out of business and liquidating its inventory. We attended the auction and came home with a four-poster bed, a Queen Anne dining table, and—best of all—a Clayton Marcus camelback couch covered in an exquisite white damask fabric. (Flash forward six months to the first time baby drooled on the seat cushion and ruined the upholstery: *What on earth were we thinking?*)

Doug was sick for 16 straight days in March. His fever broke just in time for him to accompany Jennifer to her first natural childbirth class. For all the talk about relaxing completely and breathing deeply, Jennifer was beginning to feel a little nervous about her impending delivery and was glad to have Doug at her side. Unfortunately, when she tried to discuss what she was learning in class with her doctor, he became livid. "Don't tell *me* how to deliver a baby! *I'm* the expert here. I've been delivering babies longer than you've been *alive*! No, I *can't* guarantee your husband can stay in the room with you. He may get *horsy* on me, and I'll have to throw him out...." Perhaps he missed the good old days, when women were knocked out cold before giving birth. Jennifer wasted no time in finding a new obstetrician. Dr. Ben Howard graciously agreed to take her on, and we've been delighted with his clinical expertise, as well as his bedside manner.

April brought cause for great jubilation. Not only did we celebrate both our birthdays and the anniversary of the day we met, but Doug finally heard from Southwestern: "We are pleased to offer you a position in our 1988 entering class...." Glory hallelujah! We won't have to move to San Antonio, after all. (He'd received an acceptance letter from *that* branch of UTHSC back in January).

May was filled with music. While Doug despaired of *ever* learning to sing (he'd been taking lessons from Jennifer's voice teacher for over a year now—an exercise in frustration for both parties), Jennifer re-auditioned for the Dallas Symphony Chorus, now required of all members annually. She sang Mozart's *Queen of the Night Aria*. Director Ron Shirey stopped her halfway through, fearing she'd go into labor if she had to hit any more high high A's. One is enough, he assured her: she may keep her spot in the first soprano section. The Chorus performed Prokofiev's *Alexander Nevsky* mid-month. As soon as the strings began to tune, our unborn child stopped turning somersaults and settled down to listen, thus demonstrating a discriminating taste in music, even *in utero*.

The month was nearly over before baby showed any sign of wanting out. Jennifer eventually felt a few contractions, and Doug drove her to the hospital. They were more intense by the time we pulled into the parking lot, but she was still determined to deliver *without* anesthesia. Ninety minutes later, she was wondering how her friends whose labors lasted two solid days ever *survived* 48 hours of *this*. "I can't do it," she begged, "give me an epidural!" Too late, the doctor informed her. Baby is crowning, so push. That she did and was rewarded with a beautiful son: Jonathan Douglas entered the world May 31 at 3:02 AM. He measured 22½ inches and weighed a whopping 10 lbs 6 oz, with ruddy skin, dark eyes, and a shock of long black hair. His sideburns were so long, in fact, that it was all Jennifer could do to resist trimming them on the spot!

Doug began a research job at Southwestern the day after Jonathan was born. He spent the summer in the pathology lab studying rat hearts—poor little rats. Jennifer's parents were concerned about her being alone while Doug was at work and insisted that she shouldn't be climbing our apartment stairs so soon after giving birth, so we ended up staying at their house the first week of June. Doug suspects this was really just an excuse to pamper their daughter and hold their new grandbaby, but he dutifully delivered his wife and son straight to their doorstep the day they were discharged from Presbyterian Hospital.... Our dear friend and philosophy professor, Jim Parker, came over for dinner once we had moved back home. He brought two pounds of chocolate, explaining that his mother always claimed it made her milk rich. (Eager to test that hypothesis, Jennifer polished off the entire box in about three days.) Dr. Parker also brought news of Doug's biological family, having sleuthed around San Antonio with the information Doug had gathered from opening his own adoption records earlier this year.

Although his birth mother is no longer living, the rest of the family welcomed us with open arms when we made their acquaintance a few weeks later. Doug went from knowing absolutely nothing about his blood kin to having a detailed, written genealogy that dated back to the 1300's in Norway and to the 1500's in Germany—complete with photographs of the last six generations, copies of their marriage certificates, and maps of their ancestral homes! The story of his mother's death is very sad: she conceived out of wedlock, was forced to give her baby up for adoption, grieved over the separation for an entire year, and took her own life on Doug's first birthday. She wrote that she could not bear to live with the knowledge that someone else was raising her child. Tragic though it was, the story provided a measure of comfort for Doug, who had always assumed he was unloved and unwanted.

August took us to San Antonio to celebrate our first anniversary, although it wasn't the romantic getaway Jennifer had envisioned. Doug's childhood friends were home for the summer, so we spent the evening at Trek Doyle's house, reminiscing about bygone days until well after midnight. At least, *one* of us was reminiscing—the other was trying to piece together what disjointed fragments of conversation reached the corner where she sat nursing the baby. It was a little like listening to an inside joke for six hours running. The candlelight dinner and schmaltzy music would just have to wait for the next night.

September was spent party-hopping. In addition to the baby shower given to us by our friends at Town East Baptist Church, we attended half a dozen events designed to welcome new medical students, introduce them to various clubs on campus, acquaint their wives one with another, and celebrate our embarking on the long educational journey that lay ahead.

Doug attended his classes faithfully, at least until he discovered the *scribe service*, which allowed him to just read over class notes instead—something he could do much faster than actually sitting through the lectures. Jennifer took a sabbatical from her graduate studies to stay at home with Jonathan. With baby in arms for most of the day, she adapted to doing many things one-handed, including reading, vacuuming, washing dishes, and ironing clothes. Sewing and handcrafts have been more of a challenge, although in October she did manage to stitch curtains for the nursery and paint a heart-shaped welcome sign for the front porch while Jonathan was napping.

In November, Thanksgiving found us with hearts full of gratitude for our marriage, our baby, our home, our families, and our *opportunities*. Jennifer has developed an even deeper appreciation for God's many blessings having spent time this fall getting to know our new neighbors, a startling number of whom work as topless dancers to pay the rent. By day, these single moms congregate in our living room to share meals, study the Bible, and learn how to cross-stitch while their little ones play on the floor at our feet. By night, they take the stage at a downtown strip club and sell themselves cheap. It is heart-rending.

We'll be heading to Corpus Christi in December, stopping in San Antonio on our way to enjoy the bright lights and festive atmosphere of the Riverwalk. We hope your seasonal celebrations will be joyous, as well, as we remember again the birth of our Savior, the Lord Jesus Christ. May He bless you and yours in the coming New Year.

With love from the Flanders family:
Doug, Jennifer, and Jonathan

1989

This year proved to be a very eventful one for our family: in mid-January we attended a "Family Restoration Seminar" which dealt with God's intended design for family life and the role the family is to have within society. It was an excellent and very challenging study. We found out only a few days after this workshop that Jennifer was pregnant again, and it thrilled us to think that God is building our little family even faster than anticipated. What a special way this was to start the New Year.

In February, Doug transferred his church membership to Town East Baptist where Jennifer and her parents were already members. He was asked to teach his first children's sermon the Sunday he joined, and he continued to teach these on a regular basis during the months that followed. He's an animated story-teller, and the object lessons he incorporates are always lots of fun. Do you know how they trap monkeys in South America? Ask Doug. He'll tell you.

We did a little traveling over Spring Break in March, first driving down to San Marcus and Corpus Christi with Jennifer's parents and sister, then making a quick trip to Oklahoma (just the three of us). We stayed home this year for Easter, and it's a good thing we did— Jonathan cut three teeth on Easter Sunday. That made it a long day for *all* of us.

Also in March, Jonathan learned to stand alone, to whistle, and to clap his hands. By April he was feeding himself, drinking from a cup, sorting blocks, taking his first steps, and saying "mama" and "dada". He was walking by the first of June; now he runs. He can also do front rolls. His vocabulary has expanded to 10-12 words now, though he seldom uses them, preferring instead to communicate using his own contrived language: a rolled guttural "r" means "helicopter," clicking sound means "cracker," head cocked to side with palm to ear means "bed," sucking air between his forefinger and thumb means "candy," kissing his palm means "please," wiping two fingers across his chest means "peanut butter," and patting the top of his head means "put me on your shoulders, Daddy, and take me for a ride!"

We had many things to celebrate during late spring: Doug's and Jennifer's 22nd and 24th birthdays and the anniversary of the day they met (3 years ago) in April; the completion of Doug's first year of medical school, Jennifer's re-acceptance into the Dallas Symphony Chorus, Jonathan's baby dedication, and his first birthday in May.

In June, our entire family signed up for summer courses through the Mesquite community center. Jennifer and her mother took a ceramics workshop together, Jonathan enrolled in "Mom and Tot Diaper Gym", and Doug started karate lessons. One afternoon, Jonathan observed his dad practicing some of his karate kicks and later began to imitate them. Thereafter, whenever he heard the word "karate," Jonathan would immediately stop whatever he was doing and hike a leg…. Toward the end of the month, Doug's parents paid us a visit. This meant a lot to us since we so seldom get to visit with them now that Dad is pastoring in New Mexico.

Christmas is love in action. Every time we love, every time we give, it's Christmas.

Dale Evans

Jennifer's mother's family held their annual reunion in Oklahoma in July, but with the baby's due date so quickly approaching, we had to miss it this year. Those reunions are such fun. Nana was thirteenth in her family, so Jennifer has always had more cousins than she could count.

Jennifer's parents kept Jonathan for us so that we could attend the Basic Life Principles seminar the second week of August. This was Doug's first time to hear Bill Gothard. We had a tremendous time and are hoping to attend the advanced seminar together next spring.

In September, God blessed us with a beautiful baby girl—Bethany Ann, 9 lbs. 3 oz., 21 inches, born at 9:23 a.m. on the 20th. Although she was 17 days late, when it finally came time, she really came fast. She was born in the labor room. Her appearance so caught the attending nurse by surprise that she screamed for help, bringing a flood of nurses and residents into the small room. Fortunately, Dr. Howard, Jennifer's obstetrician, was among them. (At least, we think he was—*somebody* was on hand to catch the baby, and we vaguely remember seeing his face in the crowd at the foot of the bed).

From the very first few days of her life, Bethany slept six hours at a time and woke up happy. At about two weeks, she developed severe colic, causing her to cry inconsolably for three to five hours a night. We really believe that this was God's way of insuring her some individual attention, though, since she slept so contentedly the rest of the time (during Jonathan's waking hours). As a result of this concentrated time spent with our daughter, we've gotten to know her and grown to love her in a very special way. She really is a precious little girl! As an added benefit of being up with Bethany five hours a night, Jennifer was able to get a good bit of reading done, finishing 14-15 books in the course of three months (six of these were James Dobson's—all excellent, the most recent ones were Larry Crab's *Marriage Builder* and Mary Pride's *All the Way Home*—must reading for all young couples).

By October, Jonathan had learned his various body parts and would point to his eyes, ears, nose, shoulders, knees, and toes whenever we asked him to do so. He now enjoys demonstrating this same knowledge on his little sister, which leaves her somewhat bewildered. He is very affectionate with Bethany and is also very protective of her. He loves to kiss her forehead and to blow bubbles on her tummy and is always the first to her bedside whenever he hears her crying.

We made another trip to Corpus Christi in November to spend Thanksgiving with Doug's grandparents. The long drive is more difficult with small children than it was before (just try spending eight hours hunched over a car seat attempting to nurse a fussy baby *yourself* sometime), and we are consequently not able to make it as often as we'd like, but we always enjoy seeing them so much! We try to alternate holidays between both sides of the family and will therefore be spending Christmas with Jennifer's family. It's hard to believe it's already that time of year again, isn't it? We've already decorated the tree and wrapped the presents and are surprised that Jonathan is being so patient about waiting to unwrap them (though we've occasionally caught the little Grinch trying to crawl up the stairs with a couple of smaller gifts clinched firmly between his teeth). We've also driven the family around the neighborhood to look at lights. Jonathan nearly hyperventilates every time he sees a decorated house or yard.

Toward the end of November, we took the children to see *The Little Mermaid*. It was a delightful movie, the music lively and the animation beautiful. The story hinged on a deal the mermaid struck with a sea-demon, which would have cost Ariel her soul had her father not paid the price for her mistake by taking the consequences of her foolishness upon himself. We thought it appropriate that this movie should open during the Christmas season, reminding us of the price *Jesus* paid for *us*. As we celebrate His birth, it is our prayer that all would be reminded of the great provision God has made in sending Christ to die in our place. May all of you have a very merry and meaningful Christmas!

With love from the Flanders family:
Doug, Jennifer, Jonathan and Bethany

Photo by Sears Portrait Studio

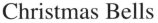

Christmas Bells
by Henry Wadsworth Longfellow

I heard the bells on Christmas day
Their old familiar carols play,
And wild and sweet the words repeat
Of peace on earth, good will to men.

And thought how, as the day had come,
The belfries of all Christendom
Had rolled along the unbroken song
Of peace on earth, good will to men.

Till ringing, singing on its way
The world revolved from night to day,
A voice, a chime, a chant sublime
Of peace on earth, good will to men.

And in despair I bowed my head
"There is no peace on earth," I said,
"For hate is strong and mocks the song
Of peace on earth, good will to men."

Then pealed the bells more loud and deep:
"God is not dead, nor doth He sleep;
The wrong shall fail, the right prevail
With peace on earth, good will to men."

1990

So much has happened to our family during the last twelve months. It has been a difficult year in many respects, but God has sustained us through it all. His grace indeed is sufficient.

Bethany continued to suffer from severe colic in early January, crying inconsolably for four to five hours a night. Some friends of ours witnessed one of these attacks and suggested Bethany might be allergic to the milk Jennifer had been drinking. Jennifer subsequently eliminated dairy products from her diet, and Bethany's colic completely disappeared. This was no coincidence: all attempts to sneak a little milk or ice cream during the months that followed would bring the colic back full force, so Jennifer had to remain lactose-free until Bethany was weaned.

In early February, our whole family became infected with a virus that lingered for weeks. Though the rest of us had recovered by the end of the month, Jonathan never fully regained his health. He frequently had abdominal cramps and was still very congested, which affected his speech (although by the first of March his vocabulary had grown to include over 35 words).

Bethany learned to pull up on hands and knees and to sit at five months. By March she was crawling. Doug had a two week break from school this spring, which he devoted almost entirely to painting the walls, building shelves in all our closets, and other such home improvements. Jennifer's Aunt Irene spent a week with us. She helped sew linens for our master bedroom during the day (curtains and a dust ruffle from a pink and green floral), then attended Bill Gothard's advanced seminar with us each evening. Jennifer had to miss the last two days of this conference as Jonathan's health worsened. His stomach pains had become more severe and were accompanied by nausea and vomiting. He had an insatiable thirst, drinking as many as six or seven full glasses of water in one sitting, which we attributed to the antihistamines he'd been taking for his congestion. Though we made frequent trips to the doctor's office, it was still not apparent what was causing his problems.

We flew to Albuquerque the first week of April to visit Doug's parents. This was their first time to see our little Bethany, hardly a newborn now at 18 pounds and 30 inches. It was our first time to see Dad's new church. When we returned to Dallas on April 2, Jonathan's weight had dropped sharply. Though he continued to drink large volumes of juice and water, he could keep very little on his stomach. What he didn't throw up would quickly pass through as urine, completely drenching his diaper, pajamas, and bed linens seven to eight times a night. We recognized the polyuria/polydipsia to be symptomatic of diabetes, but little expected that to be Jonathan's diagnosis. After contacting our pediatrician again April 10, we took Jonathan, trembling and dehydrated, to be re-examined. Dr. Gray sent us immediately to Children's Medical Center where Jonathan was admitted with Type 1 diabetes. During the six days he spent in the hospital, Doug never left his side. Though this was traumatic for all of us, Jonathan adjusted quickly to the shots and blood tests required to keep his diabetes under control (he now gets three shots and four blood tests a day). The staff did a beautiful job coordinating activities for the patients, including Easter egg hunts, visits from the Easter bunny, egg dying, painting, etc. This, coupled with all the prayers, calls, cards, and visits he received from our family and friends, made his stay at Children's a much more pleasant one. In fact, the story of his hospitalization is now one of Jonathan's most frequently requested bedtime stories. Only by the grace of God could such an initially terrifying experience be turned into such a fond memory in the mind of a two-year old.

By May, Bethany could stand up, clap her hands, drink from a cup, say "Mama," and climb our entire flight of stairs (although it took much longer to crawl up than to roll down!). She cut her first two teeth and began eating solids. The weather was getting pretty enough that we could take the children swimming in the afternoons. A pair of "water wings" enabled Jonathan to be much more independent at the pool. Doug planted a bed of periwinkles in our "front yard" (the 3'x4' patch of dirt outside our apartment door). Jennifer and the children kept them well watered, and we all watched with excitement as the first blooms appeared. Another welcome sign of spring was the one that had the words "Garage Sale" printed on it. God has used such sales time and again to provide for our needs, and He continued to do so this year. We'd hunt them as a family every Saturday morning, praying as we went, and seldom returning home empty-handed.

Some of our dearest friends, the Robbins, moved in across the parking lot from us toward the end of May, and by June we'd all begun attending the Family Sunday School Class at First Baptist Church of Dallas. This class has been such a blessing and encouragement to us. Parents and children meet together, and the fathers take turns teaching the class. It's a mixed group—we have everything from a converted Jew to a charismatic Catholic attending—but they all love the Lord and are committed to worshiping Him as a family…. Jennifer and the children signed up for summer classes through the community center again this year. In addition to the "Read-to-Me Club" and "Mom-n-Totnastics," we also took a

"Kitchen Helpers" cooking class (Jennifer had almost as much to learn in that department as Jonathan did). Doug's parents and sister came to visit us in late June, and then the seven of us flew to Corpus Christi to visit his grandparents for a few days. This was the first time our extended family has all been together in eighteen months! We went to the waterfront one afternoon while we were there and took the children for a ride on a paddleboat. Channel 3 happened to be on location filming a spot on tourism, so our family appeared on the evening news. We watched the footage on the airport terminal's television—*that* certainly kept the children entertained while waiting to board our plane.

> *Never worry about the size of your Christmas tree. In the eyes of children, they are all 30 feet tall.*
>
> Larry Wilde

Doug began clinicals in July. His first rotation was a killer: Internal Medicine. It kept him at the hospital 60 hours out of 96, and we missed him sorely every minute he was away. Knowing this, he brought home a pair of gerbils to keep us entertained in his absence (though they could scarcely do the job as well as he), and later added a couple of goldfish to the menagerie. A more significant addition to our family came mid-month when Jennifer's sister Kimberly married a godly young man by the name of Jeff Hancock. Unquestionably, it was "a match made in heaven," and we were all thrilled.

Doug and Jennifer celebrated our third wedding anniversary in August, so grateful to God for the life and love He has given us. Jonathan's sensitivity to spiritual things became more evident this month when he began offering precious, detailed prayers without our even prompting him. One evening he was thanking God for the sandbox he had at Papa's house (which Jennifer's dad had built for his first birthday), when he asked if he could "please have a sandbox at Jonathan's house." Jennifer mentioned this to her parents on the phone that evening. Within 24 hours, Papa was in our backyard building a 7'x 4' sandbox for Jonathan. Jennifer cannot recall when her dad has *ever* finished a project so *fast*. We are deeply indebted to him for showing our son that God does, indeed, hear and answer prayer!

Bethany began standing alone in August. Within days, she was walking without help. She learned to hug and kiss this month and would take advantage of every opportunity to express her affection to everyone around. She also began to use some two-word phrases and to obey simple commands. On September 20, she celebrated her first birthday. She is a "happy, happy, happy" girl and such a joy to have around.

Doug finished Medicine in September and began his OB-GYN rotation, delivering over

30 babies in the course of four weeks. You can imagine what exciting work this was for him—he absolutely loved it and would probably specialize in obstetrics were the hours not so unpredictable. Jonathan began children's choir at church this month. His favorite song is "Funny Fat Frog." Mom likes it, too, which is a good thing, since she helps teach the preschool class and the children beg to sing it (and sing it and sing it) every week. Jonathan visited the dentist for the first time this month after a fall on the concrete loosened his front two teeth and one began turning dark. The x-ray showed that the nerves to his top front teeth had died, putting the teeth at risk for infection.

Jonathan woke up one morning in early October with a completely dry diaper. Though we hadn't really planned to begin potty-training just yet, Jennifer told him that if he could stay dry for the rest of the day, she would take him to get some "big boy pants" that evening. He was successful, so Nana went with us to get some Mickey Mouse underwear at Wal-Mart. We brought them home, tried them on, and Jonathan has not worn another diaper since. Such was the extent of his potty-training! It was also this fall that our family took up cycling. We got a pair of mountain bikes, attached a baby carrier to each, and bought helmets for the entire family. This has provided hours of fun and relaxation, in addition to promoting regular exercise, family togetherness, and fuel conservation. And God has kept us safe. Once we determined those flimsy kickstands can't support a baby's weight alone, we've had no accidents at all!

In November, our gerbils gave birth to six babies. This came as quite a surprise to us as we just happened upon the tiny red litter one morning while changing their water. They've grown quickly and will have weaned by Christmas, if any of you are in need of a last-minute gift idea or are interested in giving one a good home. They'd make an unforgettable stocking stuffer. Who could forget a gerbil? (Certainly not anyone who's ever owned one of these nocturnal bundles of hyperactivity, that's for sure!)

We spent Thanksgiving in Oklahoma with Jennifer's family and will spend Christmas this year with Doug's. Jonathan had another dental x-ray the week after Thanksgiving, which revealed that the roots of both the damaged teeth had become abscessed. He is scheduled to have a root canal and caps put on both teeth December 17. He will be under anesthesia for the procedure. Please pray that the surgery goes well, free of complications.

Our Sunday school class had their annual family Christmas retreat at Mt. Lebanon the first weekend of December. While we were there, one of the children, Paul O'Keefe, Jr., suffered a severe asthma attack and died. He was only ten years old, his parents' only child. Doug was with him when he collapsed and immediately began administering CPR. He kept this up for about half an hour until an ambulance arrived. Although the boy's breathing and pulse returned three separate times during the ordeal, he ultimately was unable to survive the attack. His death serves as a tragic reminder of how fragile and uncertain life is. Indeed, each of us is but a heartbeat away from eternity. And while little Paul knew and loved the Lord

Jesus, there remain yet many who do not. As we celebrate the birth of our Savior this holiday season, it is our prayer that those who know Jesus will cling to Him and that those who do not will call upon His name while they still have the breath to do so. God bless you every one and give you a truly meaningful Christmas!

With love from the Flanders family:
Doug, Jennifer, Jonathan and Bethany

Photo by Kmart Portrait Studio

Merry Christmas!

New Year Resolutions

We are a family of list makers, and we love the fresh start each New Year gives. Even if we don't achieve all our goals, we think setting them is a good exercise that allows us to accomplish more than we otherwise might.

Many times, we will begin working on New Year's resolutions a month or so in advance. I don't mean just thinking about them, but going ahead and implementing the changes we want to make. This helps us form new habits early, so we will be more apt to succeed once January arrives.

Instead of listing vague resolutions (like "get in shape" or "read more"), we translate those goals into well-defined, bite-sized, short-term objectives, like "do 50 sit-ups before breakfast each morning" or "read at least 15 minutes every night before bed."

Here are the top items on our list every year. Maybe they'll prompt you to consider making a few New Year's resolutions of your own.

Spiritual: consistent prayer (individually, as a couple, and as a family), Bible reading and memorization (we pick specific passages to work on together with the kids.

Mental: read more (we aim for a book a week), make lesson plans (for home schooling the children), learn a new language.

Physical: get consistent exercise (aim for 15 min. a day), eat right (high fiber, fruits, and vegetables), avoid sugar (which some of us do more successfully than others).

Social: attend weekly church services, home school field trips, show hospitality.

1991

Several of our friends and family members wrote to us after Christmas last year to say they hoped our news this year would be more pleasant, so we are happy to report that this has indeed been a very good year.

January brought with it many changes for our family, as we rang in the New Year with a longer list of resolutions than in all our previous years combined. (We even managed to keep a few of them!) Doug devised a schedule for Jennifer and the kids, effective January 1st, Monday through Friday, 8-11 a.m., consisting of lessons in Scripture memorization, reading, math, art and science. The children loved having so much of Mom's undivided attention and learned quickly. By the end of the first month, Bethany's vocabulary had expanded to include 75-80 words, and Jonathan could identify a dozen written words, major organs of the human body, numbers 1-30, and scores of different bird, animal, and insect species. Our rent was supposed to have increased by $75 a month this year (our lease expired in December); however, we received a call from the leasing office toward the end of January asking if we'd be interested in answering phones for the apartments three nights a week. If we were to accept (which we most gratefully did), they would forward the calls to our home and reduce our rent by $180—effectively cutting it in half!

In February, we took a weekend trip to Tyler, Texas, with some close friends, Mary and Warren Robbins and their two children. We all had a wonderful time. The zoo there is great (free, too!) and the rose gardens spectacular (though just beginning to bloom when we visited).

We continued our travels in March, flying to Corpus Christi one weekend to visit Doug's grandparents, and driving to Oklahoma the next to see Jennifer's kin. We were back in Mesquite for Easter, in time to dye eggs with Nana and Papa and to eat Sunday dinner at their house. Lest you think the eggs, baskets and bunnies caused the children to miss the true meaning of Easter, we overheard Jonathan in the bathroom one night explaining to Bethany why Jesus was nailed to a cross: "He died for our sins, Betsy, and I just love Him so much!"

Our travels ended in April, with a one-day visit to friends in Ft. Worth. The following weekend, we attended Greg Harris's homeschooling workshop at Criswell College. Some friends of ours from First Baptist's Family Class, Fred and Sarah Cooper, have long been involved in coordinating this seminar in the Dallas area and asked this year if we would serve as exhibit hall chairmen. We were happy to oblige, and in return for our labors (which were few), we received free admission to the seminar, a $25 gift certificate for workshop materials, and dinner with Mr. Harris and the seminar coordinators.… April 10th marked the one-year anniversary of Jonathan's diabetes diagnosis. That same week, the men from our Sunday school class met in our home to pray for Jonathan's health. This was a very precious time for our family, the memory of which we will always cherish. Jonathan has adjusted very well to the management of his diabetes (he can even test his own blood now without any assistance), though he continues to pray faithfully that God will "heal my pancreas or help the doctors find a cure."

In May, we began a new reading program using the book, *Teach Your Child to Read in 100 Easy Lessons.* This approach was ideal for Jonathan, who is a very visual learner. Within just a few weeks, he was beginning to sound out words on his own. Jonathan turned three on May 31st and received a pet rabbit for his birthday. We thought the bunny seemed a little lonely and considered getting a second to keep him company, but thought better of the idea after discovering our pet gerbils had given birth to a *sixth* litter that same week.

Jennifer's parents began a big landscaping project in June, so for the following two or three months, Jonathan spent every Saturday morning at their house "helping Papa dig in the dirt." We joyfully learned mid-month that Jennifer is expecting again. This baby is due February 28th (which should put him here on St. Patrick's Day if he's as late as our last one!).

Jennifer and the kids took a break from school in July, though Doug had no summer vacation this year. He finished a rotation in anesthesiology, his field of choice, on June 28th, then began senior year courses July 1st. He volunteered to edit the course guide for anesthesia and ended up getting paid ($500) to do it! This gave him an excuse to buy a new computer so he could work on the project at home. Once that job was completed, he began the long process of requesting and submitting applications for residency programs.… Jennifer had a scare this month when her obstetrician couldn't detect baby's heartbeat and ordered a sonogram. The first images showed no baby at all, indicating a possible molar pregnancy. We had to endure a long weekend of restless nights before having higher-resolution ultrasound. This one clearly showed a healthy baby boy, and Jennifer has had no problem since. Bethany made the big switch from diapers to Minnie Mouse panties this month, toilet training with very little effort. Jonathan was quite an encouragement to her in this endeavor, cheering her on with great enthusiasm whenever he'd see her running for the potty. Toward the end of July, we returned to Believer's Chapel. With so many godly Christian families there who've successfully raised obedient children, we have a wealth of experience to draw upon as we seek Biblical counsel in matters pertaining to child training.

Doug's parents and sister paid us a visit in August. They gave us a couple of weeks forewarning, which afforded us time to complete a few neglected chores before they got here. We steam-cleaned the carpet, stripped and repainted the furniture in the nursery, reupholstered several chairs, and reviewed proper table manners with the children. (We see Doug's family so infrequently—it's especially important to us that everything be in order when we do). Quite ironically, Jonathan and Bethany both took ill the morning of the Flanders' arrival and threw up all over the freshly shampooed carpet, the newly upholstered chairs, the refinished furniture, and even on Aunt Priscilla! That was *nasty*. To top it off, the stomach virus caused them to lose their appetites, so we weren't even able to show off their table manners!

Through the months of September and October, Doug taught cell-biology labs at the school. In addition to furnishing us with some extra income, this provided a much-needed respite from the rigorous hours of clinical rotations. The hours were fantastic: weekdays 1-4 p.m. with Wednesdays and weekends off. Who wouldn't love a cushy schedule like that? We took advantage of the extra time together to enjoy some family outings. We visited the zoo, the aquarium, Science Places I and II, the planetarium, a local Putt-Putt golf course, Samuel Farm, and the State Fair. We both entered a spinach salad contest at the Fair this year. Our salads didn't win any awards, but we'd be glad to send our recipes to any of you who are brave enough to try them (we hadn't the stomach to do so ourselves)!

Bethany celebrated her second birthday September 20th, though it is difficult to believe she's only two. She's 36½" tall (completely off the chart), 29½ lbs., and has a phenomenal vocabulary (in her parents' opinion, at least!). She can sing the alphabet song in entirety, quote Bible verses verbatim, and recite countless nursery rhymes—in German, even! Of course, you'll just have to take our word on all of this, as she refuses to "perform" in public! Where's that video camera when we need it?

Jennifer's mother's family held a reunion in Oklahoma the first weekend in October. We rode up with Jennifer's parents, sister, and brother-in-law in a 15-passenger van that Nana and Papa had rented for the occasion. This made the 5-hour trip almost as enjoyable as the reunion itself! We experienced a real victory this month when the children began once again to go to bed without a fight (this had somehow become a three-hour nightly battle, in addition to the two-hour struggle we encountered at naptime). Doug interviewed at Parkland in mid-October. It looks hopeful that we'll be able to stay in Dallas for his residency, though we won't know for certain until next March. Five months and 25 lbs. into Jennifer's pregnancy, we finally got on the ball and found a new obstetrician. (Dr. Howard, whom we loved so dearly, retired from his OB practice last January.) Our new doctor's name is William Cutrer. He's a very nice, conservative, pro-life physician, of whom we've heard nothing but glowing reports. (He is also a Christian and has been attending Dallas Theological Seminary part-time for the past six years.)

Doug's grandparents sent him an early graduation gift in November—a check for a new car! We used it to buy a 1986 Plymouth Voyager mini-van. It's beautiful, well cared-for, and accommodates our growing family very comfortably. Bethany gave us a real scare this month when she fell through a horizontal brachiating ladder from six feet in the air and landed flat on her face. Her chief complaint was, "I didn't get to slide, let me try it again," but when we attempted to help her up, she could neither walk nor support her own weight. She had improved dramatically by the time we reached our pediatrician's office, but was still exhibiting some symptoms of a possible concussion—slurred speech, impaired balance, pallid appearance—so we were sent to Children's Medical Center for a CT Scan. The scan came back normal (to our great relief), but she walked with a limp for several days following the accident.

December will be an especially busy month for our family. In addition to the local Christmas programs and events we traditionally attend, we'll be going to Six Flags Holiday in the Park this year (our first time—Jennifer won four free tickets in an essay contest). Doug will have an interview in Oklahoma City and two nights of call this month. We're also planning to spend some time in Sulphur (OK), San Antonio, and Corpus Christi during his two-week break. Please pray that God will keep us safe through our travels, as we wish the same for you. May God grant each of you a most joyous and meaningful holiday season and keep us all ever-mindful of (and thankful for) His great Gift to us, the baby Jesus, which is Christ the Lord!

Photo by Kmart Portrait Studio

With love from the Flanders family:
Doug, Jennifer, Jonathan and Bethany

1992

January began at a snail's pace for us, due in part to the fact Doug was in the midst of a difficult rotation, Jennifer in the last weeks of her pregnancy, and the children on a less rigid "school" schedule. By the time February rolled around, however, things began to gain momentum.

Doug planned a nice, romantic dinner for two on Valentine's Day, but the baby was quick to remind us there were actually *three* people present. Jennifer felt a sharp abdominal pain as we entered the restaurant, and by the time we were seated (an hour and a half later) she was having contractions three minutes apart. Dr. Cutrer advised we skip dinner and rush straight to the hospital. We complied, but the contractions stopped as soon as we reached the labor room and didn't begin again for another five days. Still a week away from her due date, Jennifer anticipated a long labor and brought along *Foxe's Book of Martyrs* to read while she waited, but after only four hours of contractions, she had to lay the book aside as our little David Michael made his hand-first appearance at 1:01 am, Thursday, February 20. He weighed 9 lbs. 1 oz. (our smallest yet) and measured 21½ inches. From the very beginning, he has had the most pleasant disposition, seldom complaining about anything. He truly is a joy—always so happy and content!

Providentially, David was born just one day before Doug began a six-week vacation—we couldn't have timed the birth better had we "planned it" ourselves! So it was that through the month of March, while Mom and baby rested at home, Dad and the kids painted the town, visiting a different museum, park or local attraction every day! By the end of the month, Jennifer and David had begun to venture out with them on their excursions, and our entire family enjoyed a three-day retreat in Pine Cove with a group from Believer's Chapel.

April was birthday month for our family: Doug turned 25 and Jennifer 27. Our brother-in-law, Jeff, celebrated his 30th, though he scarcely looks it with his new braces. For his birthday, Doug received a copy of Larry Burkett's *Illuminati*, which proved to be the best fiction we read all year (the year's best non-fiction was Paul deParrie's *Romanced to Death* and Cal Thomas' *Book Burning*, which we'd highly recommend to any of you who have not already read them).

May marked the welcome end to Doug's four-year stint in medical school. He graduated from Southwestern on the 30th, and Jennifer had to blink away the tears as she videotaped him crossing the stage to receive his diploma. (We almost missed capturing this moment of family history on film—Jennifer inadvertently left the battery pack for our camcorder at home. When she realized her mistake, she fervently prayed that God would send somebody with a Sony to sit in the seat behind her, which is exactly what He did. That person graciously lent us his battery pack long enough to tape the desired footage!) Doug's parents and sister came to town for the big event, then stayed to celebrate Jonathan's fourth birthday with us on the 31st. We had an even greater cause for rejoicing earlier this month when, one evening at bedtime, our tender-hearted little Jonathan told us how sad he is when he does wrong and how much he wants Jesus to live in his heart and help him do right. He prayed that night to give his heart to God, then began the very next day sharing the good news with his little friends.

June brought with it an indication that Jennifer might be expecting our fourth baby. The symptoms persisted the entire month, during which time we did several pregnancy tests. We thought the negative results we kept getting must surely be incorrect, but they were evidently accurate. Jennifer must have just had the flu. Those five weeks of nausea and fatigue would have seemed a joy had pregnancy been the cause, but it was a disappointment to have endured it for naught. What part of June was not spent at home performing pregnancy tests was spent traveling. We made two trips to Oklahoma and also spent a couple of days in Corpus Christi. Additionally, Doug had to stay four days in Austin while he took the Federal Licensing Exam (FLEX). We were all back in town for Father's Day, and that afternoon the elders met with us in our home for a time of prayer and sharing. We are so grateful for our church family—not a Sunday goes by that we do not thank and praise God for the fellowship and teaching we receive at Believer's Chapel.

On July 1, Doug began the first year of his residency. He will be at Parkland for his three years of anesthesia, but is doing his internship year in medicine at St. Paul. He worked an average of 120 hours a week this first month. More difficult than any of us had anticipated was the adjustment to this new schedule. By the end of the month, Jonathan was wishing his dad had never graduated (his school schedule was much better than this!). During the long hours Doug was away from us, we distracted ourselves by reading. Jennifer finished Janette Oke's *Love Comes Softly* eight-book series in two weeks, and by the end of the month, Jonathan and Bethany had both logged 32 hours in the library's Summer "Read-to-Me" Program, each earning a book of his/her choice and a reading certificate. Even David got in on the action with 16 hours of being read-to; the rest of the time he spent eating (adding solid foods this month), sleeping (through the night now plus two naps), and crawling (perfect cross pattern by July 30).

In August, David got his first tooth, had his first haircut, and said his first word ("mama"); Doug was sworn into the Army Medical Reserves (he's a captain); and we put a bid on what would have been our first house (had the owners not rejected our offer). Our fifth wedding anniversary was August 15. Since we'd been spending so little time together as a family, Jonathan and Bethany celebrated with us this year. We all went to Wet-n-Wild, but ended up spending most of the evening in the kiddie pool (Jonathan insisted the big slides made him feel like he "might need to throw-up" and Bethany feared she would drown if separated from her inner-tube again). Another prayer was answered toward the end of the month when Bethany gave her heart to God. More than anything else in the world, we want our children to know, love and serve the Lord Jesus Christ, and we cannot begin to express the joy it has brought us this year to see our oldest two express a desire to do just that. While we realize Jonathan and Bethany may still be years away from having the maturity to make this decision with full understanding of all it entails, it's good to see that God is already at work in their hearts at this young and tender age.

Our sweet Bethany turned three in September, though she hardly looks 16 months younger than Jonathan. They are so near the same size that strangers often mistake them for twins. We feel very blessed to have such a loving and affectionate little daughter. Bethany is still very talkative (Papa insists that her curly hair is not the *only* trait she inherited from her great-grandmother!), so conversation seldom drags when she is around. Doug had the opportunity to demonstrate his medical expertise this month by doing a little cosmetic surgery on his wife—he removed five of Jennifer's most bothersome moles, acting both as surgeon *and* anesthesiologist. Jennifer's Dad was so impressed with his son-in-law's work that he offered to let Doug "whittle" on him, too. Word spread, and by Thanksgiving a long queue of family and friends gathered around the kitchen table after dinner, watching and waiting for their turn to be de-moled!

October took us to Oklahoma again for Jennifer's mother's family reunion. Her parents were there for four days, but the rest of us (including Jennifer's sister and brother-in-law) rode up together and stayed only two. Jeff didn't want to be away from the books any longer than that, as is preparing for the CPA exam. Of course, *Kimberly* doesn't have to study any more, since she finished her Master's degree in June…. Jennifer went under the knife again the following week, and this time Doug joined her. We both had radial keratotomies done by Dr. Charles Key to correct our nearsightedness. Thinking we'd signed up for laser surgery, we were a bit unnerved when he warned us to "keep your eyes still" and started slicing away at our corneas with those sharp scalpels; nevertheless, the surgeries were successful. We could both see 20/20 the minute we left his office, so neither of us needs to wear glasses any more. (Please note that the bulging of Doug's eyes in our Christmas portrait is *not* a consequence of this surgery, but merely a side effect of the 36-hour shifts he's been working at the hospital!) Doug had a week's vacation the end of October, and we spent two days of it at the coast visiting his grandparents. In an effort to pass time while on the plane to Corpus Christi, Doug reviewed flight-safety rules with the children. Jonathan was fascinated by how the seat cushions were designed to act as flotation devices, but Bethany was so terrified by the prospect of an emergency ocean landing that, when it came time to return to Dallas, she refused to board the plane until she had secured a promise from the captain that he wouldn't fly over any water!

Of course, November got off to a rather dismal start with the unfortunate election of Bill Clinton. Jennifer took a photograph (for posterity) of the children in front of the newsstand the morning Clinton's victory was announced in the headlines. As soon as the kids spotted Mom's camera, all three broke out grinning from ear to ear, but we can assure you they were the *only* ones in this family who were smiling! Jennifer cried for half an hour when she heard Bush's concession speech. As she lay awake fretting about the damage that could be done by such a morally-bankrupt president over the course of four years, Doug calmed and comforted her with a reminder that "He who is in us is *greater* than he who is in the world." Indeed, we have nothing to fear—our God is sovereign over all. By the end of the month, Jennifer's parents were nearing completion of their remodeling project: Mother has her new bay window in the kitchen, an atrium door in the utility room, and 33 inches added to the length of both rooms (Jonathan got to help knock out the walls). Since Jennifer's Dad is doing all the work himself, it naturally is perfect. It should really be spectacular once he gets entirely finished. Doug was off work the last week of November. We spent Thanksgiving Day in Oklahoma, but tried the rest of the time to just relax at home and enjoy one another's company.

December will find Doug spending all of his days (and many of his nights) at the hospital again. He will not have another break in his schedule until next April. Though our family will be separated physically for much of the time this Christmas season, our hearts will be united in thanking God for the wonderful gift He gave us so long ago in the person of His Son, Jesus. It is our prayer that those of you who have likewise accepted this precious gift will join us in praising Him for it, and that those who have not might come to faith now and thereby discover what is the *true* meaning of Christmas. God bless you all and grant you a most joyous Christmas and prosperous New Year!

With love from the Flanders family:
Doug, Jennifer, Jonathan, Bethany, and David

Photo by Kmart Portrait Studio

1993

What a busy, busy year this has been for our family! Doug got free tickets to see the Dallas Cowboys play in January. He and our brother-in-law Jeff cheered them on at Texas Stadium just three weeks before their super-bowl victory. It was a bit chilly, so the guys had to bundle up well to stay warm. Doug was grateful for an excuse to wear a cap, since Jennifer had slipped cutting his hair a couple days before and left him with a terrible bald spot above his left ear. It took six months for his head to fully recover!

The following month, we learned that Jennifer was expecting. Jonathan began thanking God for "little Hannah or Samuel" a couple of weeks before Mommy even started to suspect, but a test February 5 proved him right. David celebrated his first birthday February 20. He learned to wave bye-bye this month and took his first step. Within a few weeks, he was walking everywhere.

Bethany had tubes put in her ears in early March. The surgery restored her hearing to a normal range and brought a welcome end to the chronic ear infections she has suffered for the past couple of years. She was a real trooper for this procedure—even offered to let the doctor operate *again* if she could eat another donut afterwards…. Jennifer had a sonogram mid-month when, at 11 weeks, the baby's heartbeat could not be located. The ultrasound, which was completely normal, indicated this baby is another boy. When Bethany heard the news, she protested, "I love my brothers, Mommy, but I'm just a little bit *mad* at you that I don't have any *sisters*!" Jonathan decided it was time he found a job this month, so he posted a sign in our front window offering to sell advice for two cents. Unfortunately, this little business venture was not extremely profitable—he did much better during the summer months peddling original artwork and grape Kool-Aid. We spent the last weekend in March at Pine Cove for our couples class retreat. Jennifer and the kids rode down Friday with another family from the Chapel, and Doug met us there Saturday afternoon once he came off call. The weather was beautiful, and we all had a wonderful time.

We bought tickets to fly to Corpus Christi for a visit with Doug's grandparents the first weekend of April, but Jonathan and David both took ill the night before we were to leave, so Jennifer stayed home with the sick boys while Doug and Bethany went on alone. (Throughout the entire trip, Bethany kept repeating, "I love you, Daddy. I like getting to go places with you, Daddy. You're very nice, Daddy.") David weaned this month, added a couple of words to his vocabulary (for a grand total of five), and learned to follow simple instructions. Jonathan learned to ride a bike without training wheels, which has been a great source of exercise for him. He was soon riding so much that his insulin requirements were reduced by almost 40%. As has become our annual tradition, we attended the Mesquite Rodeo when it opened in April. Jonathan was determined to win the calf scramble this year, so he got a pair of new running shoes and practiced for weeks in advance. When the time came, though, he forfeited the race in order to help a younger child who'd fallen on the field. Winning isn't everything—he passed the more important test.

By May, our new baby had grown big enough that Jennifer could feel his constant kicking. With this reminder that we'd soon exceed even further our apartments' limit of two-children-per-room, we began browsing for a bigger place to live. We spotted a house May 5 that suited us perfectly and signed a contract on it two days later. One of Doug's classmates from Southwestern got married in Tulsa on the 22nd of May, so we decided to drive up for the wedding and visit Jennifer's grandmother and a couple of her aunts on the trip there and back. We'd almost made it to Oklahoma City when our Voyager broke down. A clog in the oil pump burned up the engine (note to self: never keep driving once a warning light comes on), and it had to be completely replaced. We ended up leaving the van in Norman for repairs and renting a car to get back to Dallas. We could have flown to *Europe* for what that trip to Oklahoma cost us once we'd paid for the tow truck, taxi, car rental, gas, engine repair, and one-way airfare (so Doug could drive the van back home once it had been fixed)—and we missed the wedding, to boot!

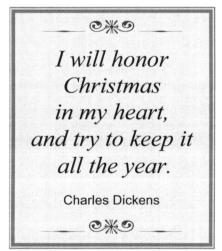

> I will honor
> Christmas
> in my heart,
> and try to keep it
> all the year.
>
> Charles Dickens

Jennifer's high school graduating class held its 10-year reunion in June. We attended, had a wonderful time, and even won an award for having the most children (our baby *in utero* served as a tie-breaker). Jennifer's parents celebrated their 33rd wedding anniversary on June 25, the same day we closed on our new house. We had already gotten Molly, our little Lhasa Apso puppy, in anticipation of having a yard in which to keep her, so it's a good thing the contract went through. We spent the last week of June getting things ready for our move: we painted the master bedroom teal green, Bethany's room pink, and the den white; had the vents cleaned, the carpet steamed, the new appliances delivered, and the house exterminated inside and out. It was hard work, but we were happy to do it.

Having finished his internship year at St. Paul, Doug began Parkland anesthesia July 1. Two days later, we packed up our belongings and began moving into our first house, which is just two blocks away from Jennifer's parents. The house has three bedrooms, two baths, one living and dining area, a galley kitchen, a separate utility room, and a double car garage. By the time we moved over the last of our stuff in mid-July, that garage was so cram-packed with boxes that we wondered how it all ever fit in that little two-bedroom apartment which had been our happy home for the past five and a half years. We were eager to sort through the mess and put it in order, but other responsibilities slowed our progress. In the midst of every-third-night call, Doug had to take the eight-hour anesthesia boards this month. (Don't you know we're proud of him? He scored 91st percentile!). Jennifer and the kids took a break from schoolwork, but continued their summer reading. When the library held its awards ceremony July 30 for the "Read-to-Me" Club, Bethany came in first place having read 420 books in eight weeks, Jonathan took second with 396, and David got fourth with 236 (he was still taking two naps a day and couldn't stay awake through as many books as his older siblings).

August was our month for mishaps. We bought a set of bunk beds for the boys' room, but within 30 minutes of our getting them home and assembled, David fell from the top and broke is left arm! He wore a splint for ten days, then a fluorescent orange cast (his color choice) for three weeks. The accident brought an abrupt end to his finger-sucking habit—the cast prevented his getting the fingers of his preferred hand into his mouth (those fingers on the right side just don't taste the same). A few weeks earlier, he chipped his front tooth while climbing off his dad's weight bench, so we made an appointment for him to see the dentist at the same time his brother and sister had their check-ups. David's tooth was fine, but the incisors Jonathan damaged three years ago had become abscessed again, despite a root canal and multiple caps. (It's a small miracle such a diagnosis was even possible, considering the fact it takes six adults to pin Jonathan down for an x-ray. Those bitewings and lead aprons elicit quite a gag reflex in that boy). He had to have the teeth pulled, but was fitted with a partial plate once his gums had healed. Jennifer developed a painful kidney infection this month, and David endured two and a half weeks of chronic diarrhea. We were kept so busy hopping from doctor to doctor, there seemed to be little time for anything else. We did manage to plant two pecan trees in our back yard and to hold a garage sale. Jennifer and the

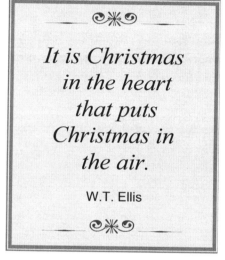

It is Christmas in the heart that puts Christmas in the air.

W.T. Ellis

kids went to Fort Worth to ride the Tarantula Train with two girls form the Chapel and their children (one of many delightful field trips we enjoyed with these friends through the summer), and our entire family (including Nana and Papa, Aunt Kimberly and Uncle Jeff) attended Ringling Brothers Barnum and Bailey Circus while it was in town. Doug's parents (recently retired and living in Bandera again) came up for a four-day visit mid-month. They kept Jennifer company on our sixth wedding anniversary while Doug was on call at Parkland.

Jonathan (5) and Bethany (4 this month) began kindergarten at home in September. We are concentrating primarily on the *Three R's* this year, though we do read a variety of science and history books from the library (Jonathan considers himself too mature for children's picture books anymore and insists on making all his selections from the junior non-fiction section). The children have developed a real love for Laura Ingalls Wilder's books, so we've been reading several of those, too. We finished the fifth in her *Little House* series this month. September was also a great month for finishing home projects as we raced the clock to get as much as possible done before the baby was born. We painted the kitchen walls, tile, and counters white to match the cabinets Jennifer had painted back in July. In the front flowerbeds, we planted new boxwood shrubs and set out two dozen red begonias. Jennifer's Aunt Irene brought her machine and spent three days sewing things for Bethany's room. She made the bed skirt and ruffled pillows in pink gingham while Jennifer stitched the curtains and comforter from a Waverly print of large pink and yellow roses on a wide, dusty blue stripe. Doug built two sets of freestanding bookshelves and a *fabulous* workbench for the garage. Then, after emptying the last of the moving boxes (hallelujah!) and tearing down the existing piecemeal shelves, hooks, and miscellaneous boards, we sheetrocked the exposed studs, then painted the garage walls and ceiling white and the floor Victorian blue. With those projects completed, we took a break, as did our air conditioner. The temperature was 90 degrees indoors, and we didn't feel like working up much more of a sweat until the AC was repaired (blessings upon Jennifer's father, who coaxed enough life back into our old unit to keep it running a few more weeks until we could have it replaced)! The only big job left to do was wallpapering the hall bathroom (mint green stripes with a lavender and pink floral border). After Jennifer prepared the walls, her dad came over to show her how to hang the paper. The bathroom's so tiny, he finished the *job* before he finished the *demonstration*. Still, she learned a lot by observing his meticulous attention to detail and was able to paste up a border the next morning without incident, thereby completing our list of projects *and* the month of September. Thanks be to God for the time and strength He gave us to get it all done!

Doug had requested to take his vacation the first week of October, knowing that the baby was due at that time, but Parkland scheduled him for every-other-night-call that week, instead (!). He was on duty when Jennifer's contractions began, got off just in time to drive her to St. Paul's and witness the birth, then worked another 24-hour shift before bringing his wife and baby home from the hospital. God blessed us with another healthy son, Samuel

Christian Flanders. He was born at 2:55 Saturday afternoon, October 2, weighed 9 lbs 3.4 oz, and measured 21 inches long. He is a beautiful baby and so very sweet! He is also very well loved by his family. Jonathan is becoming an old pro at caring for younger siblings. Even David has been surprisingly gentle with his new brother. He has recently learned to kiss and delights in so expressing his love for Samuel. Whenever he sees Samuel awake, he runs to fetch a pillow, then sits patting it in his lap, waiting for his turn to hold the baby. If Bethany were still disappointed at not getting a sister, she certainly didn't voice it. Her only complaint now is that *she's* not the mommy—"that way I could hold Samuel whenever I want!".

We really had to shift gears after Samuel's birth, but by November things were beginning to settle back into somewhat of a routine. The baby was a little fussy in the evenings, so we held and cuddled him and used that time to read some of the books we'd neglected in the months following our move. We finished Larry Burketts's *The Coming Economic Earthquake* within a few days of each other. In addition to stimulating some interesting discussions, the book prompted Doug to accept a moonlighting job in For Worth

practicing general medicine at a primary care clinic in his "spare" time. He also took a second moonlighting job working six-hour shifts at a Dallas radiology clinic. READERS' DIGEST sent us a $400 check this month for an item Jennifer submitted to "Life in These United States" almost two years ago. The story is printed on page 82 of the December issue. Doug and Jeff ran in "The Human Race" at the Dallas Zoo November 13th (Doug's first 10K—part of the marathon training he began this fall). Doug got his wish for a "real dog" mid-November when we rescued a friendly black Lab named Midnight that our neighbors were taking to the pound (a fate we postponed only for a few weeks—just long enough for the dog to demolish a couple of pillows and potted plants and to dig up the flowerbeds). He was bad about jumping our fence, but the neighborhood children always brought him back. Those kids weren't the only ones watching out for our dogs—a neighbor lady whom we'd not yet met showed up barefoot in the freezing rain one night to warn us that Molly might get sick if we left her out in the cold. She came back the following day and dressed Molly in a sweater, then the next day she brought Molly a windbreaker, a blanket, and a brand-new, fully carpeted doghouse! Doug had Thanksgiving

Photo by Kmart Portrait Studio

Day off, so we flew to Corpus Christi to spend it with his family. It snowed in Dallas while we were gone; our plane was one of the last allowed to land before DFW shut down.

December promises to be a full and joyous month for our family, if we can manage to survive Doug's augmented work schedule. Christmas is such a glorious time. We pray God's richest blessings and most abundant joy for each of you as we celebrate again the birth of His Son and our Savior, the Lord Jesus Christ. Peace be to all of you and a prosperous New Year!

With love from the Flanders family,
Doug, Jennifer,
Jonathan, Bethany, David, and Samuel

Fantasy Fudge: A Flanders Family Favorite

3 cups sugar
3/4 cup unsalted butter
2/3 cup evaporated milk (small, not large; evaporated, not sweetened condensed)
1 12-oz package of semi-sweet chocolate chips
1 7-oz jar of marshmallow crème
1 cup chopped walnuts or pecans
1 tsp. vanilla

Combine sugar, butter and milk in heavy 2-1/2 quart saucepan; bring to full rolling boil, stirring constantly. Continue boiling 5 minutes over medium heat, stirring. Remove from heat, stir in chocolate until melted. Add marshmallow crème, nuts & vanilla. Beat until blended. Pour into a well-greased 13 x 9-inch baking pan. Let cool thoroughly, then cut into 1-inch squares. Enjoy!

1994

This has been a great year for trying new things. January found Bethany sporting a new hairstyle after she used a pair of Mom's sewing shears to snip off her curls *at the root*! Doug began the year with a new job, having taken a six-month leave of absence from his anesthesia residency to practice general medicine three days a week. His new schedule provided plenty of time for family, with hours left over for working on secondary goals, which Doug summed up in the motto "READ, WRITE, AND RUN."

David turned two in February. For several months prior he'd expressed an interest in toileting, so we gave him some training pants for his birthday. Size 4T, they fit loosely enough that he could get them down all by himself, a skill he took great delight in demonstrating. His first day in the new britches, Jennifer took the children shopping. Going out with so many little ones in tow can sometimes be very taxing, but on this particular occasion all four remained unusually calm and quiet. They were so beautifully behaved, in fact, that their mother couldn't help but feel a surge of pride as she wheeled her way through the store. Heads turned on every aisle as she strolled past, and she could almost hear what all those smiling customers were thinking: *Look at those angelic children! How does that dear mother manage them so well?* Just as Jennifer was about to be swept away by a deluge of imagined praise, an elderly woman drew her attention to the fact that David (who'd been partially hidden from Mom's view by brother Samuel) was standing in the shopping cart with his pants around his ankles! He'd been mooning the entire store (thank God he was still clean and dry)!

Doug and Jonathan flew to Albuquerque to visit Doug's sister Priscilla the first of March. The trio spent tow days on the slopes in Sante Fe (the boys' first time to ski). When asked how they enjoyed it, Jonathan told us, "Dad was pretty good, but not as good as me." (He's not only honest, but humble, too!) We signed up for spring classes at the community college, which began this month: Doug took a novel writing course, and Jennifer studied writing for children. Doug's grandfather was hospitalized briefly mid-month, so Doug flew to

Christmas Games

We love to play games as a family, and there are several games and activities that we traditionally enjoy at Christmas time. Here is a sampling:

➢ **Christmas Charades -**
If you don't have a store version of this game, make your own. Put holiday-themed phrases on index cards, like "A Christmas Carol" or "Frosty the Snowman," then let the kids take turns drawing a card and acting it out.

➢ **Jigsaw Puzzles**
We keep several puzzles with holiday themes to do this time of year. Our favorites are the "family puzzles," which have pieces in three different sizes so that all ages can work it together.

➢ **Word Games**
Pass out paper and pens, set a timer, and have everybody make as many words as they can from the phrase "Merry Christmas" or "Joy to the World."

➢ **The Hat Game**
We play this game all year long, but it is especially good when we have a house full of guests at Christmastime. All ages can play. Each person writes a word or phrase on a slip of paper and puts it in a hat. The slips are then all read aloud, and players take turns guessing who wrote what. If you guess correctly, that person is out and you get to guess again; otherwise, the person you missed on gets a turn. Last left out wins.

Corpus Christi with David to visit him. A week later, the entire family gathered there for Easter. We stopped in San Antonio on our way to the coast and toured the Alamo, visited friends, and spent a day at Sea World with Doug's parents. It was a wonderful and long over-due vacation for us.

By April, Samuel was crawling, saying "mama," and eating solid foods. Spurning all the cereals and strained foods we proffered, he opted instead to cut his teeth on Nana's pot roast. David was talking more by this time, but the word we heard most often was "outside?". He learned to climb our chain-link fence this spring. Quick and agile, he could be out of our yard, down the alley, and over a neighbor's fence in a matter of seconds. We built a wooden swing set/fort in an effort to interest him and the older children in staying in their own backyard. The ploy was successful; in fact, it interested the *neighborhood* children in staying in our yard, too. David also learned to operate the switch to our automatic garage door opener this month. One bright Saturday morning, his Daddy heard a cry for help and, upon investigating, found David hanging by his fingertips from the ceiling of the garage! He'd apparently caught a ride up on the moving door, but was uncertain how to get back down. What a handful this child who was such an *easy* baby has suddenly become—making up for lost time, no doubt!

Doug and Jennifer attended Arlington's Home School Book Fair in May. We continued schooling the children through the summer, and by fall both Jonathan and Bethany had completed *100 Easy Lessons* and were reading well. We took a quick trip to Oklahoma mid-month to visit Jennifer's grandmother and great-aunt. Jonathan turned six and had his yearly check-up the end of May, but his pediatrician was concerned he hadn't grown enough (Bethany was a full inch taller). Since this is a sign of poor diabetes control, we increased his number of insulin injections from two to four daily and began testing his blood more frequently. His new endocrinologist was very pleased with this regimen and asked that we keep Jonathan on it permanently, which we have done with favorable results.

Bethany won first place in Albertson's coloring contest in June. Coloring is her favorite pass-time, next to reading and playing dress-up…. Doug and our brother-in-law Jeff ran another 10K this month. Jennifer, impressed by her husband's fabulous physique, decided to follow his example and began jogging herself. By the end of the summer, the two of us had lost a combined total of 50 pounds (25 each). On the subject of losing things: five short weeks after the appearance of his first tooth, Samuel lost his balance while standing alone, fell, and knocked it out. Ouch! *David* fell off a riding toy earlier this year and killed the nerves to his top two teeth, turning them gun-metal grey; and, of course, *Jonathan* lost those same teeth subsequent to a fall on the sidewalk when *he* was two. Apparently, perfect teeth were just never in the plans for these little boys of ours!

In July, Doug extended his leave from residency and signed a contract with University Medical Group for 50 hours a week. His plan is to delay the specialty training until our school loans are paid off. He staffs a clinic in the heart of Fort Worth's cultural district two days a week, so Jennifer and the kids began riding out with him a couple of times a month to tour the area museums while he worked. This makes for some long days when Doug is kept late on his 11-hour shifts, but it has been very educational. We spend most of our time at the Museum of Science and History, but have also visited the Kimball, Amon Carter, Cattleman's Museum, Log Cabin Village, the Botanic Gardens, Museum of Modern Art, and Trinity Park, where we rode the zoo's miniature train. The older children took swimming lessons this month. After just two weeks of instruction, Jonathan was jumping off the diving board into ten-foot water, and Bethany was sliding down the flume into the five-foot end. The younger boys played in the splash area during lesson time. David learned to hold his breath underwater, and even Samuel gained a sense of independence by cruising the inside perimeter of the wading pool…. We took the training wheels off Bethany's bike this month so that she and Jonathan could accompany Doug when he ran. She soon tired of it, but Jonathan persevered, biking up to four miles at a time with no break. He is cautious enough that we now allow him to ride from home to Nana and Papa's house unsupervised. (Speaking of Nana and Papa's, Jennifer's parents finished remodeling their formal dining room this summer, and it is exquisite: deep burgundy walls with lacquer stripes, white crown molding, plush new carpet, floral window treatments, and some of the most beautifully ornate furnishings we have ever seen.) Doug and Jeff stretched their running distance to eight miles this month, but Doug laid aside his hopes of being ready for December's White Rock Marathon, as further training for it would prove too time-consuming. Jeff was in agreement with this decision, since he'd been working over-time himself after a recent job promotion and was currently spending his spare time house-hunting with Jennifer's sister, Kimberly…. Toward the end of July, our dog Molly delivered six puppies. This was not entirely unexpected, since two months earlier the children had let a stray poodle into the yard, thinking he would "make a good friend for Molly." Moments later, an hysterical Bethany ran screaming into the house that the dogs had gotten tangled up and that Molly was about to be killed! Jennifer went outside to remove the offending pooch from our property, not realizing what an *impossible* task she was undertaking. After various and vain attempts to separate the two, and despite the clever coaching we received from our watchful neighbors, we left the dogs to work it out on their own (no pun intended). Their healthy pups arrived 59 days later and quickly captivated the hearts of our children. There were five blondes and one black; we kept the odd one (Jenny), thinking she would "make a good friend for Molly."

> *Christmas is not a time or a season but a state of mind. To cherish peace and good will, to be plenteous in mercy, is to have the real spirit of Christmas.*
>
> Calvin Coolidge

Doug and Jonathan attended the Institute of Basic Life Principles in August. This was Jonathan's first time, and we were very pleased with all he learned during the weeklong seminar. The following week, Doug returned to Corpus Christi—this time, it was Nanny who'd been hospitalized and Bethany who accompanied Dad on the "friends fly free" flight. Doug's sister, having moved back to Bandera this summer, drove down and surprised Doug by picking him up from the airport. Doug made it back home in time to celebrate our seventh anniversary. He took Jennifer shopping for her gift—a new bathing suit—and then we enjoyed a quiet dinner (alone!) at Outback Steakhouse. Jennifer's dad's family came to town mid-month for cousin April's wedding. As we made our way from the church to the country club for the reception, we spotted Jennifer's tuxedo-clad uncle standing at the corner of a busy intersection waving a tattered cardboard sign at the passing motorists. Its hastily scrawled message read, "NEED HELP. DAUGHTER JUST GOT MARRIED AND I'M BROKE. CONTRIBUTIONS APPRECIATED."

September got off to an emotionally traumatic start when Jennifer inadvertently *left David at a garage sale* (she had strapped him into the van seat, but he somehow slipped back out unobserved as she was loading the other children)! We'd driven half way home before it was discovered he was missing. Suddenly, everything seemed to be moving in slow motion, with the exception of Jennifer's heart, which had by this time gone into fibrillation. She spun the van around and started back toward the scene of the crime, weaving her way through traffic that was neither cooperative nor sympathetic, all the while praying at the top of her lungs and envisioning the horrific things which could at that instant be happening to her precious child. Meanwhile in the back seat, Jonathan sat in stunned silence, dumbfounded that his mother could pull such a prank, while Bethany sobbed repeatedly, "Oh, Mommy! David was such a *good* brother, too!" Praise be to our merciful God, when we finally made it back to the sale, we found David alone and unharmed, playing merrily in the front yard. He hadn't seemed to notice his abandonment (nor, thankfully, had anyone else) and was truly the calmest one among us. His poor mother, on the other hand, was permanently shaken and breaks out in a nervous sweat upon every remembrance of the incident! Bethany turned five on September 20. She began tap and ballet lessons this month, as did a homeschooled neighbor, Caitlin Comer. This little girl was the topic of a short (read: two sentence) creative writing assignment Bethany did which the DALLAS MORNING NEWS subsequently published in an article devoted to the topic "best friends."

We drove to Heavener, Oklahoma, the first weekend of October for Jennifer's mother's family reunion. Samuel turned a year old while we were there. He'd been walking barefoot for two months by this time, so we gave him a pair of new shoes for his birthday. Shortly after our return home, we were visited by a couple of car thieves, although we didn't realize it until the Mesquite Police rang our doorbell at 5:00 a.m. one morning to inform us they'd arrested the culprits. The thieves had been through both our cars and the garage, but had only taken the automatic door opener and Doug's electric razor. The latter was recovered by a keen-eyed neighbor who'd spotted it down the street while taking his morning walk. Doug's dad took a few days away from his new pastorate in Burnet, Texas, this month so that he, Mom, and Priscilla could come visit and attend the State Fair with us, though our outing was cut abruptly short by torrential rains. For the first time in seven years, Jennifer was neither pregnant nor newly post-partum at fair time, so she was finally able to enter her wedding dress in the fair's sewing contest (the bride must model the gown for the competition). Having spent hundreds of hours tediously hand-sewing 12,000 pearls and sequins on the gown, it always seemed a waste to wear it only once. She was glad for an opportunity to put it on again, even if the back did get buttoned a bit crooked-y in that crowded

I wish we could put up some of the Christmas spirit in jars and open a jar of it every month.

Harlan Miller

dressing room. There were lots of gorgeous dresses competing this year, but Jennifer's took first place. She suspects this was not really because hers was any prettier than the others, but because the judges were so impressed that she could still squeeze into it after giving birth four times over!

Doug's grandfather passed away November 7 at the age of 89, just three weeks after suffering two massive strokes. He was a wonderful man and will be missed terribly. Doug renegotiated his contract with University Medical Group for 40 hours a week effective this

month (Wednesdays and weekends off); however, between his frequent trips to Corpus Christi during Poppie's illness and the 24 hours of continuing medical education conferences he's had to attend to keep his license current, it was several weeks before we "realized" any extra time together. Jonathan and Bethany continued playing soccer this month on teams from our home school group, although flooded fields and runny noses caused them to miss about half of the season. In anticipation of the upcoming holiday entertaining we'll be doing, Doug and Jennifer got busy and completed a few projects we'd not had the prior motivation to finish. Doug glazed the ceramic tile floor he'd laid earlier this year in our hall bathroom. Jennifer sewed some sways for those bare living and dining room windows and made half a dozen new pillows for Bethany's bed. We also got rid of our dining room table and the four chairs that regularly fell apart whenever we'd lean against the backs of them, and purchased a sturdy oak set which will seat ten to twelve comfortably and safely. Jennifer found some clearance fabric for 73 cents a yard and used it to decorate the boys' room. She covered blankets for the crib and both bunk beds and sewed shades for the windows in blue plaid with bright yellow lining and cherry red accents. She also painted a mural of Noah's Ark over the crib (to cover the spots where the plaster peeled off the wall after she removed the posters she'd previously hung there). The boys were thrilled with the lively new colors after having lived so long in a pale blue and white striped nursery full of little lambs! We spent the week before Thanksgiving decorating the house for Christmas. We found two small trees for the children's rooms at a garage sale (25 cents each), so the kids trimmed those themselves while Mom put up the big one. Thanksgiving Day took us to Mema's house in Oklahoma. All but three cousins were there this year—including nine great-grandchildren who had an absolutely tremendous time exploring hills of rocks and sand together and playing ball with their dads and granddads.

After much agonizing over whether to go back and finish residency training or to stay out and pay off school loans, we received crystal clear direction from God, via the Army, and Doug will be returning to Parkland's anesthesia program in January (it was that, or spend the next eight years in Bosnia). Having been responsible for treating as many as 66 patients a day at the clinic, he is really looking forward to working with just one at a time again. Meanwhile, we have this one, last, "call-free" month of December to enjoy together, which we plan to do to the fullest. We hope each of you will savor the season as well. May God grant you all a joyous and meaningful Christmastide.

With love from the Flanders family,
Doug, Jennifer, Jonathan, Bethany, David and Samuel

New Year's Resolutions We All Should Make

1. Smile More
2. Spend Less
3. Stay Active
4. Don't Worry
5. Eat Smarter
6. Pray Harder
7. Hug Your Family
8. Count Your Blessings
9. Listen Before Speaking
10. Admit When You're Wrong

1995

We had high hopes for accomplishing great things this year, but when Doug returned to his anesthesia residency January 3, it quickly became evident we needed to re-evaluate our priorities. The seven pages of "Goals for 1995" Jennifer had outlined a week earlier were reduced to two main objectives: 1) *survive* and 2) preserve some *vestige of sanity*. This we've managed to accomplish, for the most part, but only by the rich and abundant grace of God!

Our tireless David turned three in February. Almost overnight, he progressed from saying single words to speaking in complete paragraphs. He loves to "read" books, work puzzles, eat popsicles, and explore the great outdoors. He's a cheerful helper, although his *unsupervised* assistance is somewhat counterproductive (as when he fed our fish this month by pouring a full cup of milk and dropping half a pimento cheese sandwich into their 20-gallon tank—the fish pulled through, but it took three months for their water to clear!).

Doug's mother was hospitalized with a collapsed lung in March, which has unfortunately been a recurrent problem for her all year. Jonathan and Bethany went with Doug to Burnet, Texas, to visit her and to see Granddad's new church and parsonage. Doug had ten days vacation this month—just enough time for a stomach virus to make its rounds through our family. We spent an uneventful week resting in bed, tending sick children, and polishing our card game. Dallas had a terrible hailstorm toward the end of March that totaled every roof in our area. Providentially, it hit while Jennifer and the kids were out of town, thus sparing our new Chevy Astro van any hail damage. Doug was on call at Parkland all weekend and therefore unable to attend our church's "family retreat" at Pine Cove, but the rest of us went on without him, stopping in Tyler on our way to see the magnificent Azalea Trails. They were absolutely breathtaking. Although Jennifer has lived on the same street for thirty years now and has no desire to leave, she found herself hoping that if ever she did have to move, it would be to a place like Tyler.

Doug became editor of *Anesthesia Airways* (the department's monthly newsletter) in April. He also began a two-month rotation through Zale Lipshy Hospital that proved to be even more time-intensive than Parkland! Despite the grueling schedule, he set aside enough time on his off-call nights to read aloud J. R. R. Tolkien's *The Hobbit* and *The Lord of the Rings Trilogy*, much to the delight of Jennifer and the older children. He kept us mesmerized through all 1800 pages of this brilliant tale, sending shivers down our spines with the creepy lisp of "Smeagol" and making us smile with the singsong voice of "Tom Bombodil." Jennifer's aunts came to town the end of the month for their yearly "sisters reunion" with her mom. Uncle Herbert drove over from Fort Worth to see them and brought along some great new educational software for us to use with the children. Thanks to him, our kids are already more computer-literate than their technologically backwards mother.

May brought heavy and persistent rains, causing some of the worst flooding Mesquite has had in over 30 years. The children insist that next time the waters start to rise, we should

all camp out in the new tree house Papa built for them in his backyard. Even before it was finished, Bethany and Jonathan began riding their bikes over every afternoon to play in this three-level stronghold. Our 12-year old Honda bit the dust this month, so Doug was able at long last to get the car of his dreams: a new, emerald-green, full-size Chevy truck.... David took a tumble on Jonathan's skateboard and broke his left thumb.... Jennifer redecorated our second bathroom using 50-cents worth of paint and wallpaper she'd bought at a garage sale. She sponged the lower half of the walls wedgewood blue, then pasted up an early American floral border at chair-rail height.... Jonathan turned seven May 31. He is such a responsible boy—I don't know what we'd ever do without him, although it looked as if we'd surely find out a couple of weeks earlier when we had our house exterminated. Jonathan complained that the fumes made him feel light-headed and went rollerblading to get some fresh air, but was nowhere to be found come lunchtime. We spent over an hour combing the neighborhood for him, and when that yielded no clues, we were *frantic*. Doug raced home from the hospital, while Jennifer dialed 911. After the operator had deciphered a very emotional account of what was wrong and had dispatched several police units to come investigate, she asked, "Have you thoroughly searched the house?" Of course, we'd already looked *everywhere*, but to humor this woman, Jennifer checked inside again. She was utterly dumbfounded to find Jonathan sound asleep in his room, where he'd apparently been the entire time. He seemed confused to wake up amid so much hysteria, but he'd have really been bewildered had he woken earlier to an empty house while his delirious family was out beating the bushes for him!

June was filled with the usual summer fare: yard work, swimming lessons, book club, and Vacation Bible School. Jennifer planted over 200 flowering bulbs and perennials in front of our house this year, only *six* of which actually *bloomed*. Doug learned to do a 1½ flip off the diving board—something he's wanted to try since junior high, but only now found the nerve to attempt. Each of our three oldest children took a turn spending the night with Uncle Jeff and Aunt Kimberly, who had by this time gotten settled into the new, four-bedroom house they bought last December…. David got his first bicycle this month. We had no idea he could even *ride* a bike until he hopped on a 16" model at Sportstown one evening, pedaled to the front of the store, and parked in front of the cash register!

July took us to San Antonio for Doug's ten-year high school reunion. This time, we won the "Fertile Myrtle" award without even having to count the baby-on-the-way. Jennifer's parents, brave souls that they are, came along to baby-sit. They rode down with Jennifer and the kids Friday morning, and then Doug flew in to join us after work that evening. Those of us on the road stopped in San Marcus to visit Wonder World and shop the factory outlet mall. There was time for more sightseeing in San Antonio between Doug's class-sponsored activities. We saw the Alamo, went to the zoo, strolled the Riverwalk, toured the Buckhorn Museum, explored the Japanese Tea Garden, and spent a fun-filled, 12-hour day at Sea World. We stopped in Burnet on our way home to feast on some delicious home-grilled hamburgers with Doug's parents and sister.

Bethany finished ballet lessons, Jonathan began baseball, and Jennifer taught Samuel's Sunday school class in August. We celebrated our eighth wedding anniversary this month, albeit a few days late due to Doug's call schedule. We really can't complain, though. Parkland's anesthesia program was put on probation this summer for "overworking residents" (a glaring understatement) and for requiring them to do too much trauma: the consequent changes that have since been made to the program have resulted in more tolerable hours, if only for a few rotations.

Doug began OB anesthesia in September. He routinely deals with such bizarre cases at Parkland that he is seldom surprised by anything that happens there. Nevertheless, he was fairly shocked this month when a patient grabbed his hand during a contraction and bit his finger so fiercely that he bled for half an hour! Thankfully, the woman was free of communicable diseases, but we had to sweat a three-day wait for her test results to come back…. Our precious Bethany turned six this month. A thoughtful girl with a tender conscience, she was baptized this summer as testimony of her faith in Jesus. She is also a voracious reader, which enables her to stay right in stride with Jonathan on his second grade studies. The two of them played on the same soccer team this fall, although Bethany really prefers dolls, dancing, drawing, and dress-up to sports.

Our towheaded Samuel turned two on October 3. He is a meticulous child, careful to keep doors shut, drawers closed, gates latched, and toilet seats down. Regardless how many snaps, buttons, or zippers are on the pajamas he wears to bed, we often find him stark naked in his crib the next morning, calling loudly for his socks and shoes, please (Heaven forbid he should face even a warm day barefoot! This his parents—who wear imitation Birkenstocks or nothing at all—can scarcely comprehend). We attended the Texas State Fair this month, as Jonathan had an award-winning Lego assembly on display there, but between Jennifer's advanced stage of pregnancy and Samuel's new interest in toilet training, we spent as much time hunting restrooms as we did viewing exhibits. Our little Benjamin Noble joined the family October 16. Although this labor was much longer (16 hours) than any of our previous ones, it was easy enough that Jennifer was able to finish a couple of needlework projects and do some light reading in the midst of it. She spent the rest of the time napping and playing cards with Doug, who'd been graciously excused from his call duties at Parkland so that he could be with his wife at St. Paul. Benjamin was our second biggest baby yet: 9 lbs 10.6 oz and 22 inches at birth. He already has those ebony eyes that are so distinctive of our Flanders boys—they turned brown before we ever left the hospital.

Jonathan and Bethany resumed their studies in November after a two-week post-partum break. David, being MUCH TOO BIG now for afternoon naps, began joining his older siblings at lesson time, working through a little pre-K curriculum of his very own. All three of them have been very good about lending a hand with household chores, as *Mom's* hands are occupied with Benjamin for much of the day (or at least they were until Daddy got the baby swing out of the attic!). We spent Thanksgiving Day in Oklahoma with Jennifer's family. Nana double-buckled with David so that we could all ride up together, and Benjamin slept the entire trip.

Another December is upon us now, and what a splendid month it is! We love the music, the lights and decorations, the festivals, the home shows, the parades and pageants and concerts. Jennifer and the kids will be singing in our church's Christmas program again this year. Samuel belts out his own version of one carol with grateful enthusiasm: Jesus "came down from heaven to *diaper* (die for) our sin!" The Chapel Singers will be presenting Part 1 of Handel's Messiah on December 16 at 7:30. We'd love for any of you who are in town to come and hear us. Although much of the gaiety of our family traditions and seasonal celebrations springs from our spending time *together*, the true *joy* of Christmas has as its source *Christ Himself.* To those for whom this is a very difficult or lonely time, we wish the deep comfort and peace that comes only from knowing intimately the Savior whose birth we commemorate. God grant us all a meaningful and joyous Christmas, and may we grow in His grace throughout the coming year.

With love from the Flanders family:
Doug, Jennifer, Jonathan, Bethany, David, Samuel, and Benjamin

- Tips for Taking Decent Family Portraits -

1. Coordinate clothing colors for a more put-together look. Solids work better than busy patterns.
2. Set up tripod and arrange shooting location in advance to minimize wait time for hubby & kids.
3. Pick one pose and stick with it. Take multiple shots to increase odds that all eyes will be open.
4. Bribe kids to smile. Give them $1 or take them out for ice cream if they smile for every picture.
5. Don't' worry if baby won't look at the camera. As long as she's not wailing, count it a success.
6. Save the last shot for funny faces. Cross your eyes. Stick out your tongue. Be silly. Have fun.

Let it snow! Let it snow! Let it snow!

We get snow so infrequently in Texas that we celebrate anytime it shows up. White Christmases are especially rare where we live. I only remember it snowing on Christmas Day twice in my entire life, and both times our family had to drive north to see it. So, whenever it does snow, we milk it for all it's worth. Here are some of our favorite ways to make snow days memorable:

❖ Take lots of pictures, especially when the snow is new and undisturbed. Tiptoe around from the back, so your footprints won't show.

❖ Bundle up warm and go for a walk. Hold hands and don't fall!

❖ Go sledding—cookie sheets, pieces of cardboard, and skateboards with the wheels removed make good makeshift sleds in a pinch.

❖ Make a snowman. Better yet, make a whole family of snowmen.

❖ Divide into teams and have a snowball fight, but no throwing snow in other's faces.

❖ Make show ice cream. Gather clean snow in a bowl and top with a mixture of 1 cup sugar, 1 tablespoon vanilla, and 2 cups of milk (plain or chocolate). Yum!

❖ Put blankets in the dryer to fluff before going outdoors. When you come back in, you can wrap up in them and get warm fast.

❖ Build a roaring fire in the fireplace. Relax around it for story time, once you are all exhausted from play.

❖ Drink plenty of hot cocoa or steaming apple cider to warm yourself from the inside out.

1996

New Year's Day found Doug in bed with the flu (his only day off all month!); nonetheless, he chose that day to begin reading C. S. Lewis's *The Chronicles of Narnia* aloud to the family. It took us four months to finish all seven books, then three more to read the lesser-known but masterfully written *Chronicles of Prydain* by Lloyd Alexander. January marked the beginning of a couple of other "just for fun" projects, as well. Doug and Jennifer collaborated to create a little comic strip, "Dr. Zork," which now appears monthly in *Anesthesia Airways* (the departmental newsletter which Doug edits at Parkland). We also began collecting marriage advice from couples who've been married 50 years or longer, for a book we hope to publish in the near future. If you know anyone who qualifies, please help us out by passing along a copy of the enclosed survey to them. They'll be in good company should they choose to participate—our most recent responses came from George Bush, Billy Graham, and Charlton Heston.

February brought snow, which thrilled even the biggest "kids" in our family. We built two squatty snowmen in the front yard and did some cardboard sledding on the bank of a nearby creek. We must have played outside too long, though, because three of the children came down with ear infections the following week. Bethany's tubes had fallen out, and she became so congested she could barely breathe. The series of visits to Dr. Kirkham which ensued ended two months later in the operating room: Bethany had her tonsils and adenoids taken out, new tubes put in, and a frenulectomy for good measure (although, she's always talked so much, few people would believe she was ever "tongue-tied" in the first place). David's tubes and tonsillectomy followed in May. As if we hadn't enough ENT trouble already, our two-year old Samuel lodged a Lego up his nose this month, then got a raisin stuck in the same nostril a week later. Fortunately, Mom was able to retrieve both items herself, thanks to a steady hand and Sam's patient cooperation, but we were told that *Doug's dad* crammed a *tinker-toy* up his nose at that age and had to go to the hospital to get it out!

March took Doug to Florida for an anesthesia conference. We arranged for our oldest four to stay with family and friends so that Jennifer and the still-nursing baby could fly to Orlando to join him for the weekend. Benjamin's nighttime colic summarily erased any illusions we might've had of this being a "second honeymoon" (it's a good thing the first one's never ended!), but we had a delightful time touring EPCOT and MGM together, anyway. Doug's anesthesia class elected a new chief resident while we were out of town. Doug was one of five doctors nominated for the position by the faculty and staff, but he didn't get the spot. His initial disappointment over the news soon gave way to relief over not having to shoulder the extra responsibility during what already promised to be a hectic final year.

Doug cut a sweet deal on some fresh horse manure in April—ten dollars for a heaping truck load! The stench was a little stronger than we'd anticipated, and we had to remove a few corncobs when we spread it on the front yard; but our neighbors forgave us once the air had cleared, and it *did* make for a plush, green lawn this summer! Our impatiens were magnificent this year—Jennifer finally clued-in to their need for regular watering, and it really paid off.... Benjamin began "combat crawling" (elbow over elbow) this month. Dragging his belly on the ground didn't seem to slow him down a bit, but it eventually forced into retirement most of the hand-me-downs that had served his three older brothers so well. We realized we could spare his clothes all this wear and tear by letting Jonathan teach him to use a skateboard. It might have worked, too, had the baby's fingers not gotten tangled up in the wheels. It took *four months* for his nail to grow back! Our almost eight-year old Jonathan began giving his own insulin injections this month after meeting a diabetic girl his age at the playground who does the same. This, and the near-constant attention he gives to keeping his hair neatly combed, reminds us that his childhood is steadily slipping away. He was baptized April 21 (his mother's 31st birthday). His favorite pastimes include leading "Bible Clubs" for his siblings and neighborhood friends, working out with his dad (in their matching muscle shirts), and hand-feeding the nearly-tame squirrel who visits our pecan tree several times a week.

May got off to a trying start: Doug worked horrendous hours doing cardiac anesthesia. Jennifer developed laryngitis and lost her voice for two weeks. Our dog Jenny bit a carpet cleaner and had to be quarantined at the city pound for ten days. Our toilet overflowed with the regularity of Old Faithful. And the kids juggled ear infections, runny noses, conjunctivitis, and a stomach virus all month long. Despite these *and other* setbacks, we managed to make a few fond memories this month and enjoyed a little culture at the same time: Jennifer's parents joined us for a free, open-air concert presented by the Dallas Symphony Orchestra at the Arboretum. Doug and Bethany attended the Fort Worth Ballet's performance of *Cinderella* after a father/daughter dinner date. And our entire family took a historical tour of downtown Dallas in a horse-drawn carriage. We returned later for a closer look at the impressive herd of bronze cattle that now stampedes through the heart of our city. It was here that Jennifer, in a *spectacular* show of grace and coordination, fell headlong into their watering hole. She avoided drowning, but could not escape the embarrassment of having onlookers cheer and applaud as she clambered out of the pool soaked to the skin!

We spent the first weekend in June camping out. Doug was on call at the VA and couldn't leave town, so we stayed in our own backyard. All seven of us piled into a new "four-man" tent, snuggled beneath our quilts, and drifted off to sleep after listening to Doug read several chapters of *Watership Down* by lantern light. The older kids finished baseball practice and spring swimming this month. David (now four) was old enough to participate in both sports this year, much to his delight, but his biggest accomplishment of the season was beginning to read. He got a crew cut this summer (as did Doug and Jonathan) which, coupled with an inch and a half sudden growth spurt and his post-surgery weight loss, caused more than one neighbor to stop and wonder who the new kid on the block was. David's energy and curiosity are as boundless and insatiable as ever. He reminds us of Rudyard Kipling's *Rikki Tikki Tavi*, the bright-eyed little mongoose whose motto is "run and find out". His career plans currently vacillate between firefighting, zookeeping, doctoring, and exploring space, but of one thing he is *certain*: when he gets big, he wants to grow a *mustache*.

> *When we recall Christmas past, we usually find that the simplest things— not the great occasions—give off the greatest glow of happiness.*
>
> Bob Hope

Jennifer was invited to sing the national anthem at an Independence Day parade in North Dallas in July. The children decorated their bicycles with red, white and blue streamers and joined in the procession, wearing patriotic T-shirts they'd made the week before. Doug marched, too, pulling Ben in a wagon, despite the fact he and Jonathan had stayed out until 2 a.m. the night before watching a midnight showing of the newly released *ID4*. We missed seeing much of the Olympics this year, but we did stage a few summer games of our own, including a competitive round of cherry pit spitting which Doug won easily with a distance of 39 feet. While our summer activities may not have garnished us with any gold medals, they were not without rewards: The kids earned a stash of books, swim passes, rodeo tickets, golf games, and free yogurt and hamburger coupons through the library's summer reading program. Doug was given a handsome bonus for scoring 97th percentile in the nation on the seven-hour anesthesia boards (his second year in a row to do so). Jonathan and Bethany won $20 cash in the State Fair's

Christmas Morning Breakfast Casserole

This dish has been the centerpiece of our Christmas breakfast for as long as I can remember. I usually serve it with a fruit salad and some hot blueberry muffins. Yum!

INGREDIENTS:

12 eggs
1 cup half & half
2 cups diced ham
1 cup grated cheddar
   cheese
2 chopped green onions
2 tablespoons dry
   mustard
salt and pepper to taste

DIRECTIONS:

1. Preheat oven to 375F.

2. Mix everything in a bowl.

3. Pour into well greased a 9x12 inch rectangular baking pan.

4. Bake at 375F until the eggs are firmly set and golden brown on top, about 25-35 minutes.

folk art competition and $75 merchandise from Crossings for their original book illustrations. David got a free copy of Disney's *Aristocats* video in a *Dallas Child* drawing. Samuel won four tickets to Six Flags and a 10-piece chicken dinner in a Grandy's coloring contest. Jonathan received free passes to Ringling Brothers Circus through a Subway promotion. And Jennifer won tickets to a Dallas Stars game at the grand opening of Baylor Mesquite.

Doug had a week off in August, so we drove the family to Arkansas, bringing our child-care reinforcements (a.k.a. Nana and Papa) with us. We spent three lovely days in Hot Springs golfing, boating, shopping, hiking, and sightseeing. Our antiquated 386 suffered a major malfunction this month, giving Doug the excuse he needed to upgrade our computer system. Jennifer's Uncle Herbert was later able to resurrect the desktop, but Doug had already bought a portable Pentium by then. The timing on this purchase was really providential, as just a couple of weeks after we got the new system on line, we were given the opportunity to begin evaluating educational software for a Dallas radio station. Jennifer may now be heard *live* every Thursday night at 7:30 on KSKY (660 AM) or via the Internet at www.cyber-line.com. In exchange for her weekly ten-minute program, "Schooling with Software," we get to *keep* all the programs she reviews. Thus it happened that David was sitting in his mother's lap one evening trying out a new CD ROM, while Samuel stood patiently at his elbow watching and waiting for his turn. After so passing a tranquil half-hour, the silence was suddenly shattered by hysterical wailing from both boys. David insisted his brother had bitten him, unprovoked, and pointed to the teeth marks on his arm as proof. When Jennifer questioned Samuel, all he would say (between sobs) was, "...but, Mommy... I wanted... something... to *eat*!" Evidently, he had fallen asleep on his feet and dreamed it was dinnertime (thought you can tell by looking he hasn't slept through *many* meals). Next to creating large messes and telling knock-knock jokes, *feeding himself* is Samuel's favorite hobby. He offers the same earnest prayer before every meal ("God... *thank you* that we're *eating*!") and devours everything left within reach. We already consume seven gallons of milk, ten loaves of bread, and 20+ pounds of produce every week. How will we ever keep the pantry stocked once these boys reach their teen years? Sam's not the *only* one with a hollow leg in this family, either. One afternoon, not half an hour after lunch, David came in from outside munching on a suspicious looking bread roll. When Mom asked where he'd gotten it, his little eyebrows shot up in excitement and he answered proudly, "*Molly* [our dog] brought it home. It's good!" Happy as we are that these little ones aren't picky eaters, perhaps it wouldn't hurt if they were a *little* more discriminating in their tastes.

Doug's long hours had begun to catch up with him by September. One week after a family dinner at Chili's, post-call, he excused himself to go to the restroom. He washed his hands and waited five minutes for a stall to empty before realizing he'd entered the ladies room by mistake! You can imagine his complete embarrassment when the person he'd been waiting on turned out to be a woman! Actually, Doug's school schedule did not demand as

much of his time this month as his job search did. Although graduation is not until next June, many medical groups are hiring early. Doug had nine interviews, each of them lasting six to eight hours. (Some of these practices were so large, it took that long just to make the rounds and meet all the partners). Bethany turned seven on September 20. She still has a passion for reading and writing, and continues to spend most of her spare time in one of those pursuits. She also loves to sing and to be sung to, and believes that no day is complete without a back rub and a lullaby before bed.

Our little Sam-I-Am turned three in October. He has definitely reached that age where it's important he do things *all by himself*. To this end, Doug took him shopping for some Velcro shoes he could fasten without help. *Who but a man* would buy size 12 shoes for a size 8 foot, thinking they'd be easier to get on and off? Jennifer wasted no time in exchanging them for a better fit, and Samuel can still manage to put them on without our assistance. Benjamin celebrated his first birthday and received his first haircut this month. Mom had to trim it a little shorter than she'd intended after Samuel planted a juicy wad of chewing gum in the middle of baby's crown. Walking early gave Benjamin a new sense of independence, but he keeps a firm grasp on Mother's apron strings, rarely letting Jennifer out of his sight without a fiercely indignant protest. Despite his being such a Mama's boy, the first word to cross his lips was "Daddy." That hardly seems fair, considering all the stinky diaper changes and late night feedings Jennifer has had to endure, but she's tried to be mature about it and forgive him this show of ingratitude.

November found us struggling again with raspy sore throats, insane work schedules, and backed-up plumbing. Fed up with the frequent floods, Doug finally installed a brand new toilet in our hall bathroom. This one works like a charm. (Would that America had reacted similarly at the polls to the mess Clinton's made of things!). Doug turned down four job offers in Dallas this month to sign with a group of anesthesiologists in Tyler, Texas. We're excited about living in Tyler, but sad to be leaving behind our wonderful family and friends. We want all of you to come visit us once we have settled into our new home. If you'll drive out in April when the azaleas are in bloom, you'll understand why we fell in love with this town the first time we laid eyes on it.

December is here, and it looks as if we my actually finish this residency and live to tell about it! We're keeping our moving plans and preparations on the back burner until after the holidays, but come January we'll be putting our house on the market and beginning to hunt for a new one. If you know anybody who'd like to live on a cozy little *cul de sac* in Mesquite (the *tenth safest city* in the United States, by the way) have them give us a call. Doug's family will be spending Christmas in Mesquite with us this year, as we spent Thanksgiving in Oklahoma with the Cowans. This will be Jennifer's first attempt at preparing a big holiday dinner, so keep us in your prayers! She'll probably play it safe and serve pot roast, be it that she's working with a culinary handicap. If that doesn't satisfy everyone, we could always turn

Molly loose and see what kind of grub *she* can rustle up! In the meantime, we send our most sincere wishes to you for a merry and meaningful Christmas and pray God's richest blessings upon you and all of yours throughout the New Year.

With love form the Flanders family:
Doug, Jennifer, Jonathan, Bethany, David, Samuel, and Benjamin

Photo by Jane Wall

- Count Your Blessings -

by Cole Porter

When I'm worried and I can't sleep
I count my blessings instead of sheep
And I fall asleep counting my blessings

When my bankroll is getting small
I think of when I had none at all
And I fall asleep counting my blessings

I think about a nursery and I picture curly heads
And one by one I count them as they slumber in their beds

So if you're worried and you can't sleep
Just count your blessings instead of sheep
And you'll fall asleep counting your blessings

1997

What a year of change 1997 has been for us! It brought a new job in a new town, a new house, a new church, a new son, new friends, new neighbors, and will soon yield a new niece or nephew, as Jennifer's sister and brother-in-law are expecting their first baby any day now. And while I'm thinking about it, you'll find enclosed our new phone number, new address, and new e-mail—so please update your directory. We'd love to hear from you!

We put our house in Mesquite up for sale by owner the first of January and sold it 16 days later, but not without a steady stream of prospective buyers first passing through our doors. We met some very interesting characters during the course of those two weeks. The most unforgettable was a 60-year old bleached-blonde who wore huge false eyelashes, drove a car like Cruella de Ville's, and came to see our house despite the fact she was violently ill at the time. We made it as far as our dining room before she lost her cookies, *spewing* them all over our walls, cabinets and floors. It was *incredible*! Despite our best disinfecting efforts, our entire family was wrenching from the same virus within the week. Before it hit, we showed the house to a newlywed couple who returned two hours later with a contract in hand. They loved the house, but were willing to wait until July to close, which meant we only had to move once. What a provision from the Lord!

Our illness lingered into February, slowing us down long enough to complete Samuel's potty training, which we had somehow neglected in the press of our normal routine. The boys were still sick when time came for the mother/daughter Valentine brunch that Jennifer and Bethany hostess annually. Rather than have us expose our guests to so contagious a bug, Jennifer's mother suggested we use her house for the party this year. It went so well, she's already planning to have us back *next* year, so the tradition needn't die after our move. It's always such a delight to have so many little girls gathered together and to watch how *quietly* they visit and how *carefully* they eat—in stark contrast to the brood of active boys that surrounds us the rest of the year!

Our five-year old David has matured so much in recent months, it's hard to believe he is the same child who in March used Mommy's razor to shave off his bangs, then cemented his eyelashes together with bubble gum. We weren't sure whether this was some desperate cry for attention or merely a re-enactment of a Sunday school lesson on Samson, but to play it safe, we promptly scheduled some "together time" for him and Dad. The two of them flew to Corpus Christi on Palm Sunday to visit Doug's grandmother. David's coming along seemed to revive Nanny's failing memory, as he is the spitting image of his father at that age.... Mesquite's Bank One was held up this month by a group of armed robbers who led the police on a merry chase before abandoning their get-away car fifty yards behind *our house.* Police choppers and news services swarmed above our roof and squad cars zipped down our alley for days on end as they attempted to track down the fugitives. Our boys begged to go out and help hunt for the criminals, but we kept them inside all week with the doors and windows locked, instead.

Doug turned *thirty* in April. He made his radio debut this month, filling in for Jennifer one week on "Schooling with Software." Cyber-line moved to WBAP NEWS/TALK 820 this year, so we can now be heard live in 38 states every Sunday night at 7:45. We still get tons of free educational software for doing this weekly review; consequently, the kids keep our computers running almost non-stop. David and Samuel have been known to get up as early as 3 a.m. to have first shot at a new program.

Jonathan and Jennifer made a small claim to fame in May when their home school research project on chain letters was published in Scholastic's national magazine, *Dynamath.* I'm sure this periodical has a terribly limited readership, but that didn't keep our heads from swelling when the editors called from New York to request photographs and an interview, which they published with the article. Doug received a flattering request himself this month when Osler Institute phoned about 10 p.m. one night and asked if he would teach part of an anesthesia review course *the following morning*! It seems that three of their guest lecturers had cancelled at the last minute, and one of Doug's professors from Southwestern recommended him to fill in. Doug tried to decline, but was eventually persuaded to drive to DFW in the wee hours of the morning and review the material himself before conducting a three-hour question and answer session on it.... We closed on our new home in Tyler the end of the month. We'd noticed a sale sign in the yard last November, but the house was taken off the market before we could get a look at the interior. Providentially, our realtor knew the owners, so after we'd searched for six months without finding anything, she managed to get us an appointment to see this house that had first caught our eye. It's about 30 years old and suits our family perfectly—a large, shaded, corner lot with plenty of space for the children to play, a wonderful floor plan with all four bedrooms on the same end of the house, three full baths, a newly remodeled kitchen, and lots of great storage. Our sweet friends from Believers Chapel gave us a lovely going away party before our move and presented us with a beautiful handmade tablecloth that is to be signed by everyone who visits us in our new home. The few signatures we've accumulated thus far look sort of lonesome, so we hope you'll make plans to come see us soon and add your name to the collection.

Doug finished his residency in June with a cardiac rotation at the VA. He was supposed to have three-day weekends all month, which we'd planned to spend in Tyler, but that didn't pan out. Jennifer and the children ended up spending several days a week in Tyler without him. We repainted three bedrooms, eight closets, a storage room, and the garage before having new carpet laid at the end of the month. We would never have finished were it not for the gracious help of our dear neighbor, Valerie Comer, who rolled walls until her arms were numb, and of Jennifer's dad, who added extra shelves and rods to all our closets, then prepped and painted the entire garage floor by himself. When Doug finally *did* get a long weekend, we decided to spend it in Arkansas. (This gave Jennifer a break from the paint fumes and reassured the children that their stressed-out mother hadn't turned into a *total* crab). It was a very relaxing trip, although we had a difficult time extricating our luggage after being rear-ended at a red light in Hot Springs. The photos Jennifer took at the scene to document the damage came in handy when the girl's insurance company balked at paying for our repairs. What really got the adjuster's attention, though, was Doug's response to her question whether we had any witnesses. "As a matter of fact, we did," he told her calmly. "We had *myself*, my *pregnant wife*, our *five young children*, and their *two elderly grandparents*, all of whom were sitting in our new Suburban when this teenage girl plowed into us." The company cut us a check the same day. June 27th was the date of our big move. The packers spent 12 hours loading all our worldly goods onto their truck, drove to Tyler, then spent four more unloading. Everyone was exhausted when the last box came off the trailer at 3 a.m. There was still a lot of work to be done, but Doug was so excited to have *this* much behind us that he went straight out the next morning and invited some of our new neighbors over for a barbecue dinner *that same afternoon*! Thankfully, they were gracious guests and pretended not to notice the fact that we had boxes stacked to our eyeballs in every room of the house and that Jennifer couldn't locate the silverware in a single one of them.

Doug brought home a documentary on the life of Evil Kineval in July. (If you've ever wondered who in their right mind would check out all those obscure titles at Blockbuster, now you know). He never stopped to ponder the effect such a film would have on these boys of ours. Sure enough, Jonathan was up at the crack of dawn the following day, constructing bicycle ramps out of scrap lumber and trying to persuade his little brothers to lie down between them while he jumped over! We quickly established some basic ground rules (like "No ramping over *people*") and then let them have their fun. These things became a magnet for the neighborhood children, and the boys made several new friends as a result, including three Tyler police officers who happened upon the ramps while on bike patrol and decided to give them a try. When they realized we were in our yard at the time and had been watching them, they grinned sheepishly, explained that they were "still kids at heart," and commended Jonathan on the fine job he'd done building the ramps. While the boys were outside on their bikes, Bethany was inside with her books: she read over two dozen *Mandie Mysteries* this summer, often finishing a book a night. She doesn't limit herself to just reading fiction, but will absorb *anything* she can get her hands on. This habit turns a simple chore like putting away groceries into a long, drawn-out ordeal, as she feels compelled to peruse the label on every purchase before placing it on the shelf.

> ❧ ✳ ❧
>
> *The best of all gifts around any Christmas tree is the presence of a happy family all wrapped up in each other.*
>
> Burton Hillis
>
> ❧ ✳ ❧

Inspired by the art of Mary Englebreit, Jennifer worked several months on a colored pencil drawing to enter in the State Fair this year. She finished it in August and took it to Dallas to be judged. The attendants took one look at the picture—that of a rested father holding a quiet toddler on his knee and reading aloud to his smiling wife and a roomful of attentive children—and insisted it belonged in a different category. They re-classified it as *fantasy*! Isn't that a sad commentary on home life in the nineties? Even so, the drawing took first place in its class, which pleased Jennifer greatly. She tackled a couple of other big projects this month, as well. She sponge painted the walls and put up a bird dog border in Jonathan's room, repainted and lined the insides of the kitchen cabinets, and put up new wallpaper in the kitchen and breakfast room. Jennifer has never had edema through six pregnancies, but her feet were so swollen after *that* job that she could barely fit into her sandals!

We spent an unbearably hot Labor Day at Six Flags in Arlington with Jennifer's parents. We dressed all the kids in matching, bright yellow T-shirts to make them easier to corral, but we should've put one on *Papa*, because *he's* the one who kept disappearing into the crowds. Nana said she was grateful we had to "keep up with five children and only one grandfather, instead of five grandfathers and only one child!" As if counting heads were not enough responsibility, we were also trying to keep track of several bags of paraphernalia, as Doug insisted we pack an umbilical cord clamp, his Swiss army knife, and a stack of bath towels "just in case." When Jennifer's contractions began as we were leaving the park and grew stronger as we traveled, we thought we might actually need to *use* those items; however, we ended up making it home before she delivered (with ten days to spare). Our little 9 lb 7 oz Joseph Tyler arrived promptly on his due date, September 11. Jennifer's labor began at four, we got to the hospital at five, had the baby at six, and Doug reported for surgery at seven— just like clockwork! Doug finished the one case that had been scheduled that morning, then took the next *five* days off. Joseph has the prettiest blue eyes, which as yet show no sign of changing color, and the longest little fingers, which he laces together whenever he nurses, as if he were saying his prayers. Bethany first saw him do this when he was but hours old. "Look!" she called to her brothers, "Joseph's saying 'Thank you, God, for giving me such a sweet and loving family.'" But Papa contends he was really asking God to protect him from this mob of siblings who were all clamoring to hold him at once! Believe it or not, Joseph was not the *first* baby to join our family this month. That distinction goes to an 8-week old puppy whom the children named "Lucky" (as in, she was "lucky" it was their push-over father who'd taken the kids shopping that day, and not their pragmatic mother). Doug was told at the pet store that she's an Australian heeler and will grow to be a mid-size dog. Naturally, he took their word on this, never mind the fact she looks just like a German shepherd and had outgrown our Lhasa apso by the end of the month. Jennifer was concerned that Lucky might overwhelm our youngest ones with all her playful advances, but the children soon proved they could hold their own against the dog. When Lucky was tormenting Benjamin one morning by repeatedly licking his face and relentlessly tugging at his clothes, Ben finally got fed up and *bit the dog* square on the back. Lucky thought twice before approaching him again...and since the *second* bite, she's left him alone completely!

> *Our hearts grow tender with childhood memories and love of kindred, and we are better throughout the year for having, in spirit, become a child again at Christmas-time.*
>
> Laura Ingalls Wilder

Samuel turned four in October. Still an early riser, he springs out of bed every morning at the first hint of dawn and bounces down the hall chirping, "De sun is up, ev'ryone! Y'all need to det up, tuz de sun is up!" (indeed, it's impossible for anyone to sleep another minute once *this son* is up). Samuel is also quite a Daddy's boy. We swam almost daily this summer, and Sam insisted on staying in the deep end with Doug every time we went to the pool. He didn't have to see too many of the gainers and double flips his dad was doing off the board before he was ready to try that himself. A new life jacket boosted his confidence, and within a week he had learned to do a perfect back flip and a fairly good front. Our gentle Ben celebrated his second birthday this month. Our pediatrician told us if Benjamin hadn't at least a three-word vocabulary by 18 months, we ought to be concerned. Not to worry, he knew *four* by then! I don't know whether the quietest children get into the greatest mischief or if they just get blamed for a larger share of it, but when all our sinks, tubs, and toilets started backing up this fall, the plumbers had to flush out our pipes every afternoon for a week before we discovered *someone* had been cramming the clean-outs full of sticks and stones every morning. We assume it was Ben, as no one else will admit to it, but one of these days he is going to learn to talk and may set the record straight on this and a great many other matters.

We took a short trip to Houston in November. We spent one day in the museums and another at Astro World. We also squeezed in a little ice-skating, which was the highlight of our vacation as far as the kids were concerned. I loved watching our older children help the younger ones make their way cautiously around the rink—would that they were *always* so protective and supportive of their siblings! We were back in Tyler for Thanksgiving. On call, Doug spent the entire day at the hospital, although he did get an hour to come home for dinner. We broke with tradition and served homemade fajitas, with all the trimmings.

We'd planned to spend Christmas in Oklahoma this year, but that changed when Jennifer's grandmother died quite unexpectedly last month. A dear believer, Mema will spend Christmas at the feet of her Savior, focused on the TRUE meaning of this season in a way those of us she left behind can only imagine. To think that the Son of God would leave heaven and be born a man for the very purpose of dying for sinners—what greater reason could we have to *rejoice*? How empty and meaningless Christmas must be for those who do not know Jesus personally. As always, all of you are in our thoughts this time of year. For those of you who already know Christ, we pray His richest blessings in the New Year; for those of you who do not, we pray you might open your hearts this Christmas to receive the greatest gift of all—salvation by grace through faith. May God keep you all in His tender care.

With love from the Flanders family:
Doug, Jennifer, Jonathan, Bethany, David, Samuel, Benjamin, and Joseph

1998

Jonathan and Bethany volunteered to help Jennifer ring in 1998, as Doug spent New Year's Eve at the hospital. We drank hot cocoa and watched the neighbors' fireworks while waiting for him to get home, which he did shortly after midnight. January found baby Joseph sleeping through the night, although he was careful not to let it become a habit! Doug took time to do a little writing this month. He penned a great column about priorities, which was published in our church newsletter, and an even better one on perseverance, which wasn't. The irony is that after his perseverance piece was turned down, Doug *quit* writing altogether for about six months! Okay, okay—so he was studying for his oral boards. He passed those in April, thanks be to God, and it is a *tremendous* relief to have all that testing behind us. But now I am getting ahead of myself.

Jennifer broke her toe in February, which caused excruciating pain for the first day or two. You can imagine how dainty her size 11 foot looked in that orthopedic surgical shoe! David turned six this month and won his first speed skating race (on a technicality—he was the first to cross the finish line without taking a shortcut to get there). He is still such a string bean, we thought a made-from-scratch birthday cake might help put some meat on his bones. Jennifer exiled the rest of the children to the back yard while David helped bake a chocolate cake topped with a green coconut farm scene. It turned out good enough to *eat*! David began first grade at home this year and immediately began shortening his name to DAVE on much of his written work. I guess it saves time. A budding scientist, he loves to concoct his own experiments. One day recently, Jennifer noticed David's shirt was soaking wet and asked what he had been doing. "I've been practicing *sneezing*," he explained. "I take little drinks of water, then blow them out my nose. One sip makes two ah-choos!"

Doug began leading a small discussion group for Sunday school in March. This assignment was right up his alley, as he definitely has a gift for gab! Jennifer was invited to speak to a group of homeschool mothers this month, sharing the podium with two other ladies. She felt like her little talk was well received, until weeks later when she heard another mother comment on what an excellent program it had been. Before Jennifer could thank her for the compliment, the woman went on to ask, "Did *you* come to the meeting that night, Jennifer?" So much for making a big impression…. We finished a few projects this month—enlarging our flowerbeds, papering and reflooring the utility room, and finishing the curtains and bedclothes for Jonathan's room—all in anticipation for our first annual "Azalea Open House." We had about two dozen friends and family drive in from Dallas during the two weeks of the trail, but we hope even more of you will come visit next year. Just pack a picnic lunch on April 3 and join us in Tyler for the day!

Our homeschool support group sponsored a Civil War Ball in April. We had almost as much fun preparing for the event as we did attending—learning period dances like the Virginia Reel and the Yankee Doodle, and fashioning old prom dresses and second-hand suits into frilly ball gowns and Confederate uniforms. Doug's anesthesia orals were this month, as I already mentioned. The examination fell smack dab on his thirty-first birthday and took place in Atlanta, Georgia. Jennifer stayed home with the children and laid six pallets of grass while he was gone. The kids helped a little, but spent most of their time breaking in the new fort/swing-set we had built in our yard just before Doug left town. They even *slept* in it—or tried to, until the mosquitoes drove all but the most determined back to their own beds.

May was one stress-filled month! The pressures we were under while Doug was preparing for the boards were nothing compared to the tension we felt while waiting for the results of his exam. This was due in part to the barrage of maladies that afflicted our family about this time: Joseph's temperature repeatedly spiked to 104 degrees, Benjamin's lymph nodes swelled to the size of golf balls, David was covered head-to-toe with enigmatic red spots (bug bites from sleeping in the fort?), and the rest of us shared what seemed would be a terminal stomach virus. Even our Suburban broke down and had to have its alternator replaced. The fact that Doug took 16 days of call this month compounded the strain, but what made it nearly unbearable was the fact that all of his classmates got the news that they'd passed the boards a full week before we received any word at all. *That* was enough to make us want to do something DRASTIC! Doug considered getting a vasectomy, but we compromised and just got rid of our video player, instead! It has been years since we've had television reception, but we more than compensated for that fact with the number of movies we rented this month alone. Now we will (theoretically) be forced to find more creative ways to cope with life's trials. Unless, of course, we lose our resolve and replace the VCR—we've kept our video library, just in case! Things had settled down somewhat by the end of the month when Jonathan celebrated his tenth birthday. He took over the chore of mowing the lawn this year and has done a splendid job of it. We paid him for his efforts, and with his earnings he bought the latest additions to our menagerie—a small, gray bunny named Hazel and a spotted white one named Fiver. He even paid for the materials Mom used to build the rabbit hutch! Jonathan has such a way with animals—wild and tame ones alike seem drawn to him like a magnet. He is beginning to have the same effect on little girls. This phenomenon has not escaped the notice of his siblings. Even our pre-schooled Sam could not resist the urge to tease his brother a little, chanting that familiar old rhyme with a slightly new twist: "Two little love birds, sittin' in a tree, K-I-S-S-*LMNO-P*!"

It may come as a shock to the many folks who have counted all our children and questioned whether we fully understand what causes them, but we actually *do* know! In fact, Doug and Jennifer were asked to address that very topic before a local church youth group in June. In a culture that has so completely divorced this aspect of life from what God in all His wisdom intended it to be, it was a real privilege to get to share with these young people God's beautiful and perfect design for oneness in marriage. We made our annual trek to Hot Springs mid-month and finally got to try para-sailing while we were there—even Jon, Bethany, David, and Samuel went up on a line. It was like floating on a cloud, except that the safety harnesses made our legs fall asleep. Nana and Papa watched our littlest ones while we were in the air, but admitted it looked like lots of fun. Perhaps we can convince the two of *them* to try it next year.

Doug's sister got married in July. She gave us only three days notice, but Doug managed to get enough time off work for us to drive to Austin and meet her intended before they eloped. His name is Chris Mullennix, and we couldn't have picked a more suitable match for Priscilla if we'd tried to ourselves. Still, the trip to Austin was much too rushed for our liking. The children kept remarkably quiet and slept for most of our time on the road, which makes us wonder how we could have travelled so many miles before hearing those sirens. It was not until Doug tried to change lanes in the small town of Thrall that

Flanders Family Christmas Traditions

> Host shoebox stuffing party for Operation Christmas Child

> Christmas card assembly line

> Ring bells for Salvation Army

> String popcorn & cranberries and peanut butter pinecones to hang outdoors for the birds

> Go Christmas carolling around neighborhood or nursing home

> Reread old Christmas letters

> Quote Luke 2 from memory

> Watch Christmas movies and read Christmas books as family

> Spend an afternoon ice skating

> Make Christmas ornaments to give to friends and neighbors

> Jog in Jingle Bell Fun Run

> Work a jigsaw puzzle together

> Make fantasy fudge, sausage balls, and other tasty treats

> Drive around to see Christmas lights and drive-through nativity

we realized we had *three squad cars* in hot pursuit! Come to find out, they'd tailed us through two towns and had radioed a third to set up a roadblock on our behalf. The officers fully intended to haul us to jail, but were so relieved to find that we were not smuggling drugs or fire arms that they just slapped Doug with a stiff fine for speeding, which was admittedly well-deserved, and bade us SLOW DOWN.

Thirty-one seems way too early to be starting a mid-life crisis, but perhaps that would partly explain why Doug felt compelled in August to trade in his dependable Chevy truck for an extremely impractical, two-seater convertible. It may also bear significance that he did this the same day Jennifer discovered the first three gray hairs in his temple. Or it could be that men really *are* from Mars! Whatever the case, Doug spent all of eight weeks crammed conspicuously behind the wheel of a tiny, emerald green, Mazda Miata before coming to his senses and swapping back for an extended-cab pick-up. August also marked our eleventh wedding anniversary, and I must confess that we have no regrets in that department, *despite* differing tastes in automobiles and divergent spending habits! To his credit, Doug has learned to shop more sensibly when he's buying for Jennifer, which would explain her delight over the dandy little pocketknife keychain she received from him this month. It actually has eleven different tools which fold up inside—*that's one for each year of marriage!* We spent three days at Hyatt Hill Country in San Antonio the end of the month. We had no choice but to put our feet up and relax this vacation, as Jennifer broke yet another toe in her rush to get packed the morning we left town! We had scarcely gotten out of Tyler before the children began asking, "Are we almost there yet?" Jennifer promised each of them twenty-five cents if they could refrain from asking that question for the rest of the trip. We enjoyed at least a thirty-minute respite before Bethany rephrased the inquiry, "Have we almost earned our quarters yet?"

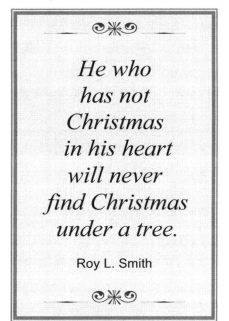

He who has not Christmas in his heart will never find Christmas under a tree.

Roy L. Smith

Bethany turned nine in September and is still the most helpful, patient, thoughtful daughter any parent could hope to have. She asked us not to spend a bunch of money on her birthday this year, as all she *really* wants is a *sister*! But, alas! She had to settle for a set of books, instead. Bethany continues to out-read us all. When her nose isn't in a book, she's writing stories of her own. Her best one to date is *Run, Lightning, Run!* told in six short but detailed chapters. Our blue-eyed Joseph celebrated his first birthday and learned to CLIMB this month. This newly acquired skill has certainly kept his guardian angels on their toes. They seem to be constantly tapping the rest of us on the shoulder, as every time we turn around, it is just in the nick of time to rescue Joseph from utter ruin! He is such an affable child, though. He tagged along to his mother's water aerobics class all summer, where he was affectionately known as "the Michelin tire baby," in reference to the inflatable inner tube in which he floated during class. Try as she might, Jennifer hasn't been able to shake off that last twenty pounds she gained during her pregnancy with Joseph. Still, she is tall and hides it well, or so she thought before seeing a former neighbor on a recent visit to Mesquite. "Wow! You've lost a lot of weight!" the neighbor enthused. Jennifer answered yes, but admitted she still had a few pounds to go, to which the neighbor sympathetically replied, "Well, it *does* seem like your *legs* are retaining water… but the *rest* of you looks great!" (Which, of course, translates: "You look like a hippopotamus from the waist down!")

Samuel turned five in October. Still an early riser, he doesn't even wait on the sun anymore, but gets up by five o'clock most every morning, just as Jennifer is putting Joseph back to bed after his first feeding. He sits quietly drawing pictures or doing arithmetic while Mom works at her desk. Samuel inherited a "cool" pair of hand-me-down jeans this summer, which has virtually become a second skin to him. He drags them out of the dirty clothes hamper first thing every morning and wears them until they are stiff enough to stand on their own. The only time they ever get laundered is when Mom forcibly peels them off his body and throws them directly into the washer. Even then, he retrieves them from the drier while they are still damp. Sam got an extra special treat for his birthday this year—an overnight camping trip alone with Dad. They left the flashlight at home, had to bum some bug repellant from more experienced campers, and lost their food supply to the raccoons, but had a great time nonetheless (for a couple of greenhorns). Benjamin celebrated his third birthday this month. Our little cuddle-bug, he gives the sweetest hugs. He loves to sneak up and kiss us when we least expect it, then dart away before we can kiss him back—a game he calls "stealing sugar" and takes great delight in playing. Ben has grown much more talkative this year, although about 90% of what he says is indecipherable to anyone outside his immediate family (the remaining 10%, *we* don't understand, either). Even so, he remains extremely patient and seems more than willing to repeat himself until his meaning is made clear! The city of Tyler built a new outdoor skate park this month, full of towering, wooden ramps on an unyielding, concrete foundation. Doug and the kids could hardly wait to check it out. After observing the ease with which the teens there did a variety of amazing stunts, Doug bought himself a skateboard and tried to follow suit. Needless to say, the tricks were more difficult (and dangerous) than they looked. On his first visit to the park after getting the new board, Doug fell and broke his left arm! This was cause for some concern, as he was in such pain the night it happened that he could hardly move his arm at all and required help to do the simplest of tasks. Even so, God was abundantly merciful and granted Doug a remarkably quick recovery. Would you believe he was able to put in epidurals for laboring women within 24 hours of taking the spill? By the end of the week, the only task at work that still gave him trouble was trying to reach behind his head to tie the strings of his surgical mask. Another physician spotted Doug in the hall the day after his accident and quipped, "I think you're gonna make out all right, Dr. Flanders, but in the meantime you ought to have someone help you comb that hair!" Doug struggled with it alone for a few more days, then gave up and got a crew cut, which he's worn ever since.

As the glorious fall weather carried us into November, our family life began to take on the reassuring rhythm of an actual *routine* (a concept totally foreign to us during Doug's grueling years in medical school and residency). After having been put on the trauma team this summer, Doug was able to cut back substantially on moonlighting and is now at home more evenings and weekends than not. That has been such a blessing! He's even had time to participate in the Tyler chapter of Bible Study Fellowship, which has been a great source of encouragement to him. Having Doug with us for dinner so many nights a week has challenged Jennifer to expand her limited repertoire of recipes. Just when it was becoming apparent that our household could not stomach many more meals of baked fish or frozen lasagna, Jennifer's friend Teresa McCarty took pity and came to our rescue. Pots, apron, and cookbook in tow, she spent over four hours in our kitchen one night teaching Jennifer how to cook—from *scratch* even! This fall, Jennifer took on the responsibility of coordinating "Mom's Night Out" for our homeschool group, which means she is in charge of planning topics and securing speakers for our monthly meetings. We have a wonderful support group here, and we've enjoyed the rich variety of opportunities it provides. The children take gymnastics, study piano, play soccer, and attend choir once a week, in addition to participating in academic competitions, going on field trips, and roller-skating once a month. Our whole family got firsthand experience in grassroots politics this year while helping with the Jim Lohmeyer campaign for Congress—rolling newspapers, walking neighborhoods, attending rallies, and manning phone lines. The children even got to shake hands with Gov. George Bush and his wife during their brief stop in Tyler. Although we are more involved in outside activities than ever before, we don't feel particularly "busy." Here in Tyler, we are literally five minutes away from any place we need to go, and our older children have become a huge help to us in everything we do. We still find time to read great books together. Doug finished C S Lewis's *Screwtape Letters* this fall, which fueled some fascinating discussions, and Jennifer is about halfway through the fourth of eight *Little Britches* books, which have proven to be rare jewels, indeed. Sterling North says that this autobiographical set by Ralph Moody "should be read aloud in every family circle in America," and we agree wholeheartedly with that assessment. Even our younger boys hang on every word of them. Most of the family—Flanders, Cowans, and Hancocks—came to Tyler for Thanksgiving this year. We crowded around the table and listened as each person in attendance recounted God's blessings, feeling overwhelmed by His goodness.

That brings us to December again. Why, this year passed so quickly that it took only three and a half pages to summarize, instead of our standard four (the smaller font helps, too)! Nevertheless, we continue to pass milestones even as this letter goes to print. At almost 15 months, Joseph finally took his first steps last Sunday. You'd think that having to crawl on hard brick floors would be all the incentive he needed to walk early, but not so. And Benjamin cast off his diapers this week (*his* idea) and started using the potty, despite his profound disinterest in doing so during Mommy's previous attempts to train him. As always, we look forward to hearing what is new with you, so please drop us a line. In the meantime, we want to wish each of you a joyous and meaningful Advent season. For our Christian friends, we pray God's continued blessings in 1999. For those who have not yet come to faith, we pray you will open your heart *today* to accept the greatest gift ever given, which is forgiveness of sin and eternal life through Jesus Christ the Lord. His grace be upon you all!

With love from the Flanders family:
Doug, Jennifer, Jonathan, Bethany, David, Samuel, Benjamin & Joseph

An illustrated version of Luke 2:

Shepherds watch their flocks.

The angel of the Lord came upon them.

And they were sore afraid.

"In the city of David, a Savior is born."

They found the babe lying in a manger.

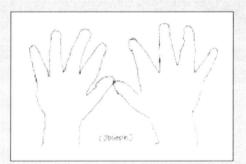

"Glory to God in the Highest!"

1999

When we told the children in January that we were expecting another baby, they could hardly contain their excitement. Bethany served Jennifer breakfast in bed for a solid week, and by the end of the month, she and Jonathan were not only doing most of the cooking, but had taken over the menu planning and grocery shopping, as well! Doug spent a week in Atlanta with the Army Reserves and brought home the flu. He recovered soon enough, but the rest of us battled it for months on end, with a few chicken pox thrown in for good measure. As if *that* combined with first-trimester-fatigue weren't enough to knock Jennifer off her feet, she broke a *third* toe last December that required surgery this month. Despite her doctor's best efforts to straighten it, her foot remains stubbornly frozen in the Vulcan sign for "Live long and prosper"—hence Jennifer's new nickname, *Alien Toes*.

Surgical procedures continued in February: Benjamin's tonsillectomy improved his speech and cured his sleep apnea, and Doug's first endoscopy revealed a hiatal hernia and a little scarring, but no colon cancer. The kids learned to skip rope this spring and practiced at every opportunity. They jumped to the rhyme, "Ice cream, soda pop, lemonade; tell me the initials of your girl friend's name," only Samuel would invariably say, "Tell me all the letters in your best friend's name," then spell D-A-D. Jennifer made Sam a black *Zorro* mask, per his request, and he handled it like an American Express card (never left home without it). We grew so accustomed to seeing that thing tied around his head—even in the bathtub—that we all but forgot what he looked like underneath! Even so, we were mortified one Sunday at church when we glanced down our row and realized Samuel had donned his disguise in the middle of the worship service. The other parishioners must have wondered about the mysterious masked man in our midst that morning…. Our snaggle-toothed David had a birthday this month and immediately went from being "almost 7" to "almost 8." He's still an enthusiastic chess player (which prompted us to start a chess club for our homeschool group) and has become an avid reader and a first-rate lawn mower, as well.

Jennifer stitched four more Confederate uniform and took all six children to the annual "Silverware" Ball in March. Doug was on trauma call and had to miss it, but that didn't keep Jennifer off the dance floor—our 18 month-old Joseph was a tireless partner and was more than willing *to lead*! We had sufficiently recovered from our string of illnesses by the end of the month to launch a massive spring-cleaning effort. It began with 25 loads of laundry in a single afternoon (we drove straight home from the laundromat and installed a lock on the little boys' closet to keep them from changing clothes 14 times a day). After Connie Reese gave her famous "decluttering" talk to our homeschool group, Doug gave Jennifer a big utility cart, hoping she'd be motivated to donate *mountains* of personal belongings to Goodwill, but not wanting her to strain her back in the process! Doug was also the driving force behind several home improvements this spring: a new roof and fresh paint for the house, an atrium door for the utility room, leather sofas for the den, and an insulated cover for the patio. Jonathan was in charge of our various landscaping projects. As soon as the daffodils had faded, he set out scores of impatiens, planted a flat of English ivy on the shady side of the house, and built a raised vegetable garden on the sunny side. The tomatoes we harvested this summer were scrumptious!

Our Top 10 Favorite Christmas Movies

1. It's a Wonderful Life (1947)

2. The Nativity Story (2006)

3. How the Grinch Stole Christmas (1966)

4. White Christmas (1954)

5. Miracle on 34th Street (1947)

6. A Christmas Carol (2009)

7. Elf (2003)

8. A Charlie Brown Christmas (1965)

9. Holiday Inn (1942)

10. Rudolph the Red-Nosed Reindeer (1964)

Jonathan ran his first 5K race with his father in April. He seemed genuinely surprised that they didn't finish *first*…but, hey, at least they *finished*! The stray cat we adopted last year had kittens this month, much to the delight of our children. When David first saw them, he exclaimed, "Oh, aren't they all so *durable*?" I think he meant "adorable," but his statement was true, nonetheless. It's a good thing, too, considering the near constant attention they received from us, and their mama's failed attempts to put them out of reach by moving them to precariously high places. We found good homes for four, but kept a striped one, who had by then become Joseph's constant companion—a role Tiger endured with patient resignation until he grew too heavy for Joseph to cart around.

Something about being pregnant always puts Jennifer in the mood to hang wallpaper (maybe the memory of Donna Reed doing the same in *It's a Wonderful Life*). It was the hall bathroom that reaped the benefit this time around—more mint green stripes, which we've missed since our move from Mesquite. Bethany's room also received a new look after she confided in her father that she's a country girl at heart and not fond of the pink roses, ribbons, and ruffles that have adorned her surroundings for all time remembered (she didn't want to hurt Mom's feelings by telling *her*). We started over from scratch—stitching new curtains and bed linens from yellow floral denim and red gingham; white-washing a new bed, chest and nightstand; and painting the walls sky blue, with a mural that surrounds the room of a white picket fence, clouds, trees, birds, rabbits, and potted geraniums. The most tedious part was painting a life-size pony on the wall beside the bed, but Jennifer saved that job until Doug and our oldest four were away for the weekend. The three-day camping trip they took in May with a group of seventy Tyler physicians and all their children proved to be a real turning point for our inseparable Sam—his fears and phobias vanished faster than his dad could pitch a tent. In fact, Samuel *himself* disappeared for a time, but without the hysteria that has accompanied such occurrences for the past year and a half. He was as happy as a lark when Doug found him, clad in a life jacket and sporting around the middle of the lake in a

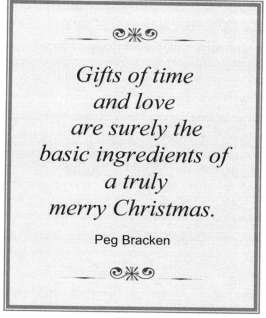

Gifts of time and love are surely the basic ingredients of a truly merry Christmas.

Peg Bracken

kayak, all by himself! David and Samuel were both baptized this month, and Doug was privileged to do the honors. What a tremendous blessing it has been to see all four of our oldest come to faith at such early ages! Jonathan turned eleven on May 31. A budding ornithologist, he combined his birthday money with his savings from lawn mowing and bought a pair of binoculars from his favorite store in the world, *Wild Birds Unlimited*. He would shop there daily if we'd let him, as much to visit with the owners, George and Cindy Ramsey, as to add to his already large collection of bird feeders.

Our nightly trips to the community pool resumed in June. Doug and the older children swam laps, but Jennifer got her exercise chasing Joseph, who was more interested in trying on all the aqua-shoes and sandals left at poolside than in getting in the water! Bethany took it upon herself to teach Benjamin to swim this summer, and he was a quick learner. Keeping his plastic-wrapped hand out of the water made paddling a little tricky, but that is what he had to do after the tip of his finger got accidentally sliced off by our back door. Having an anesthesiologist in the family sure comes in handy! Doug put a digital block in Benjamin's finger before we even left for the emergency room, so Ben remained calm and cooperative through the entire ordeal (at least until the attending physician began scrubbing the pieces to stitch back together, which was enough to make the strongest stomach queasy). The day after Ben's mishap, Joseph took a wild belly-ride on a runaway skateboard and knocked his front teeth loose. It must be something in the Y-chromosome—our boys are now five for five on damaged incisors! Fortunately, our pediatric dentist lives just a few doors down the street and offered to make a house call to examine Joe's teeth during naptime so as to avoid upsetting him when he was awake.

Our missionary friends from China paid us a visit in July, but were only here for three days—just long enough to update us on their work, demonstrate the proper use of chopsticks, and teach the children a couple of songs in Chinese. An *unexpected* guest dropped in on us the same weekend and is living here *still*—a pigeon named Ash, who was but a scraggly squab when she fell into our fireplace and got rescued by the kids. We kept her indoors and fed her by hand until her feathers grew in, then moved her outside once she learned how to fly. She considers herself a part of the family, though, and pecks on the door or window whenever she wants to be let in. She especially enjoys our evening story time and likes to perch on Doug's head or shoulder while he reads aloud…. Jonathan spent a week at a diabetes day camp this month, swimming, boating, horseback riding, and learning about the latest advancements in diabetic care. He had a blast, but must have missed us almost as much as we missed him, because he asked permission from the camp director to bring his sister along with him for the last day of camp…. We drove to Oklahoma the end of July for the Cowan Reunion, spending a night in the Arbuckle Mountains on our way up and swimming at Turner Falls, which was quite an experience. Our uninhibited children intuitively dropped to their bellies to navigate the slippery rocks beneath the falls, while their not-so-clever parents came home black-and-blue from trying (unsuccessfully) to cross on foot!

We attempted to adopt a black lab from Animal Rescue in August, but ended up sending her back, as the retriever had irreconcilable differences with our pigeon. Ash seemed relieved to see the dog go. The rest of our animals get along great with the bird. In fact, after our cat gave birth to a second litter this month, the pigeon stood guard over the four kittens round the clock, pecking relentlessly at the hand of anybody who tried to interrupt their nursing. Having survived the trauma of an early separation from her own parents, she seemed bound and determined to protect these babies from a similar fate! Our rabbits also had a litter this month. We kept the lone survivor, *Blackberry*, but are sad to report that our cats did not get along as well with the bunny as they do with the bird….

After witnessing the birth of that last batch of kittens, our older children redoubled their efforts to persuade Mom and Dad to let them see the delivery of our #7. They even slept on the couches in the den for the last two weeks of Jennifer's pregnancy—fully dressed, including socks and shoes—to be ready to hop in the truck at a moment's notice. So when our little Rebekah Lyn arrived in September (9/9/99), four of her siblings were on hand to insure she received a warm welcome. Jonathan cut the cord; Bethany and David helped weigh and measure the baby (9 lbs 14½ oz and 22¼ inches); and while Samuel kept his eyes closed for much of the birth, he evidently saw enough that he could afterwards state with conviction, "I sure am glad I'm not a *girl*!" One convenient thing about having another daughter is that we were beginning to run out of boys' names, although we were not yet desperate enough to use Sam's suggestion of *Second Samuel* (notwithstanding the fact that it is, indeed, a Bible name, as he astutely pointed out). Our resident escape artist turned *two* this month, and his blue eyes have already taken on a more mischievous sparkle. We put extra locks on all our doors shortly after Joseph's birthday, since he is prone to wander and has grown quite adept at covering his tracks! It looks as though our added sense of security will be short-lived, though…. Joseph discovered through minimal trail and error that he could push a *ladder-back* chair against the wall and climb its rungs to reach the new locks, so we know it's just a matter of time before he learns to pick them, as well! Bethany also celebrated a birthday this month—her *tenth*! We

don't know exactly when or how it happened, but she has suddenly started looking much more like a young woman and much less like a little girl. We're not the only ones to notice, either. One day this summer, Bethany was standing next to some (unrelated) toddler admiring the animals in a pet store, when a sales clerk told her not to let her *son* climb on the display case!

October was ushered in with great fanfare by a school band that rehearsed its most rousing tunes every morning at 9:00 while marching up and down our block. Our children considered this a daily parade and would pour onto our front porch at the first sound of its approach to gawk at the band members as they passed by. They had opportunity to gawk at their father this month, as well, when Doug's interview explaining epidurals to a local reporter was televised on the Tyler Evening News. Sam turned six in October and Benjamin turned four. Ben amazed us all by teaching himself to pedal a bicycle several weeks before his birthday. It had been Sam's bike and didn't even have training wheels, but that didn't slow him down a bit. Now he can ride a three-mile stretch with the rest of the family without working up a sweat…. Doug was scheduled to attend a medical conference mid-month in Biloxi, Mississippi, and decided at the last minute to take the family along with him. We stopped in Louisiana on our way to tour Vermilionville in LaFayette, the USS Kidd in Baton Rouge, and the Aquarium of the Americas and Audubon Zoo in New Orleans, then caught the Civil War battlefield and memorials in Vicksburg on the trip home. You'd expect that cramming seven children into the Suburban for an eight-hour drive might give rise to some battles of our own, but such was not the case. In fact, the kids traveled *so* well that Doug took us all back to New Orleans for a second conference the following month.

Rebekah had failed to regain her birth weight by the first of November, so we began supplementing with formula feedings every two hours. She had some trouble even latching onto a bottle at first, but eventually got the hang of it and gained rapidly—as much as eight ounces a day. The complete sense of inadequacy Jennifer felt trying to breastfeed this baby provided a keen reminder of the futility of trying to raise *any* of our children by our own strength. How utterly dependent we are upon the sustaining grace of God—whether we acknowledge it or not! Several students from the middle school across the street began harassing some of our little ones this month. They'd lie in wait until the boys came out to ride their bikes, then would chase them with sticks, surrounding them and shouting obscenities. When Jennifer heard about this, she suggested the children *stay inside* to play. When Doug heard about it, he jumped in his truck, kicked on the 4-wheel drive, and plowed across the field to where the bullies were hiding down by the creek. The little chat that ensued must have helped them see the error of their ways, because from that day forward, they would hurry past our house without breathing a word, all the while casting nervous glances over their shoulders. Needless to say, our children found their dad's way of handling this situation to be far more impressive than their mother's!

Christmas is not as much about opening our presents as opening our hearts.

Janice Maeditere

Now that December is here again, we are enjoying another benefit of having no television—*no commercials*! The children haven't been brainwashed into believing they must have the season's hottest toy or latest fad to be happy, which explains how Samuel could suggest we just give him "a paper airplane with a picture of a dog on it" for Christmas. Adults have long observed that the packaging often holds more interest for a child than the gift inside. Our older children must realize it as well, because Jonathan has asked for a box to keep his tools in, Bethany wants a box for her sewing supplies, and David requested a box for storing his Legos. Of course, our most precious gifts cannot be put in a box at all—the love of family and friends, good health, sweet memories, LIFE itself, and best of all, forgiveness of sin, and salvation by grace through faith. We pray that if you do not know Jesus already, you won't let this century come to an end before committing your life to Him in full. And for you who've already accepted this greatest of gifts, we pray you'll let God's light shine through you ever more brightly to a dark and dying world. May God's richest blessings be upon all of you in the new millenium!

With love from the Flanders family:
Doug, Jennifer, Jonathan, Bethany, David, Samuel, Benjamin, Joseph and Rebekah

Hark! The Herald Angels Sing
by Charles Wesley

Hark the herald angels sing
"Glory to the newborn King!
Peace on earth and mercy mild
God and sinners reconciled."
Joyful, all ye nations rise
Join the triumph of the skies
With the angelic host proclaim:
"Christ is born in Bethlehem."
Hark! The herald angels sing
"Glory to the newborn King!"

Christ by highest heav'n adored
Christ the everlasting Lord!
Late in time behold Him come
Offspring of a Virgin's womb
Veiled in flesh, the Godhead see!
Hail the incarnate Deity!
Pleased as man with man to dwell
Jesus, our Emmanuel
Hark! The herald angels sing
"Glory to the newborn King!"

Hail the heav'n-born Prince of Peace!
Hail the Son of Righteousness!
Light and life to all He brings
Ris'n with healing in His wings
Mild He lays His glory by
Born that man no more may die
Born to raise the sons of earth
Born to give them second birth
Hark! The herald angels sing
"Glory to the newborn King!"

2000

We tossed out Joseph's pacifier in January, hoping to wean him cold turkey, but he promptly confiscated Rebekah's to use instead. The Girl was left with nothing to suck but fingers and toes. Having thus learned to comfort herself, however, she began sleeping through the night at four months. Joseph remains a man of few words, although he once took the pacie out of his mouth at El Chico's long enough to state emphatically, "Mommy! Bekah hazzuh knife! She cud choke!" He then replaced the plug and didn't utter another word for three weeks. What he lacks in verbal skill is made up in physical prowess. By 2½, Joe could ride a bike, rollerblade, mount a trapeze, and scale a 6' wooden fence! Doug made partner in his anesthesia practice on January 1. Even more welcome than the increased income was the unlimited vacation, part of which he used right away to have a long overdue tonsillectomy. He was trading stocks at his computer within hours of the surgery, which must've kept his mind off the pain, because he never breathed a single complaint the entire two weeks he was home convalescing. Doug and the kids took the wheels off our skateboards when it snowed this month and went snowboarding down the school slopes. I'm glad they seized the opportunity while they could—the children may be grown and gone before it ever snows in Tyler again.

Jennifer agreed to sing at her parents' church in February. What she thought would be two-songs-before-the-sermon turned out to be an hour-long concert advertised in the local paper. Her father told her not to worry about her mistakes, as they served to put the audience at ease. If he's right, then that crowd was as relaxed as they get! It was fun, but she won't be quitting her day job anytime soon.... Jon worked part time for *Wild Birds Unlimited* jugging birdseed this winter. We thought he might spend most of his earnings before leaving the store, given his new employee discount, but he saved a good portion to use at Lowe's, having lately become enthralled with carpentry. He built himself a workshop in our attic, convinced Papa to install some electrical outlets, and spent the rest of the year stocking it with power tools and scrap lumber. David turned eight this month. He loves to build, too, but his preferred medium is Legos. Our decision to spend spring break at Legoland, California, was due almost completely to his lobbying efforts.

With gas prices topping $2 a gallon, March may not have been the most economical time to take a 4000-mile road trip to the West Coast, but it was ideal in every other respect. Jennifer packed enough matching outfits to color-coordinate our entire family for two weeks. Dressing alike and keeping the children between Mom and Dad when we were out (single-file, biggest to littlest) made it easier to count heads. We soon realized we weren't the only ones counting, but didn't fully appreciate what a spectacle we made until we were stopped on the crowded streets of Las Vegas by some tourists who exclaimed, "We saw your family at San Diego Zoo last Monday!" We listened to books on tape while traveling and made frequent stops at whatever points of interest lay in our path, including Carlsbad Caverns, Hoover Dam, Forest Lawn Memorial Park, and every museum we could find that granted free admission to Discovery Science Place members. Jennifer left a detailed itinerary with her mother, whose prayers we felt the whole time we were gone. Mishaps were minor and few. Rebekah got sunburned at the zoo and sported dreadful scabs across her nose and forehead for the rest of our trip. Doug swallowed a gallon of saltwater trying to surf at Carlsbad Beach, but looked terrific doing it in his $3 wet suit rental. We drove to dizzying heights to see the Giant Sequoias, but unwittingly stopped a mile short of seeing the General Sherman Tree with its 36½ ft diameter, having become distracted by the grazing deer, the melting snowdrifts, the glorious sunset—and the vomiting child in our backseat (Ben got queasy on the way up)! We survived a 4-mile hike along Las Vegas Boulevard the night we were in Nevada. Totally mesmerized by the neon lights, Benjamin walked straight into a brick wall and fell flat on his back at the feet of a street person. The bedraggled gent hurriedly passed his brown-bagged bottle to our six-year old Samuel for safe keeping, bent over, helped Ben up, dusted him off, reclaimed his booze, and sent us on our way! We did not do any gambling in Las Vegas, but couldn't leave town

> *In the old days, it was not called the Holiday Season; the Christians called it "Christmas" and went to church; the Jews called it "Hanukkah" and went to synagogue; the atheists went to parties and drank. People passing each other on the street would say "Merry Christmas!" or "Happy Hanukkah!" or (to the atheists) "Look out for the wall!"*
>
> Dave Barry

without trying one of those sumptuous buffets. The children were told to eat anything they wanted. After surveying an endless assortment of smoked meats, seafood, salads, side dishes, and savory desserts, David contented himself with two full plates of maraschino cherries and lemon wedges. There was snow on the ground in Williams, and the kids had a novel time staging snowball fights in their swimsuits around our hotel's heated outdoor pool. We took a train to the Grand Canyon, but stayed a healthy distance from the edge the three hours we were there. Mercifully, Joe (who'd been voted most-likely-to-fall-to-the-bottom) slept through most of that stop!

Rebekah learned to crawl in April. The first thing she did after becoming mobile was to track down brother Joseph and snatch back her pilfered pacifier! The pigeons nesting in our

chimney deposited two more fledglings in our fireplace on Easter Sunday. We were thrilled, especially since Ash had flown away for the winter and not returned. We named these Coal and Ember. They ate from our hands and sat on our shoulders until they learned to fly, but were never so fond of kittens or story time as their sister had been. Joseph was determined to potty train this spring, despite Jennifer's vain attempts to postpone it for a more convenient time. He changed from diapers to brother's underwear every time Mom's back was turned and spent his days trotting from toilet to toilet with his pants around his knees. His persistence paid off, and by the end of April he actually had something to show for his efforts. What's more, he figured it out for himself, right down to replacing an empty roll of toilet paper with a full one when he's finished! I wish he'd teach that trick to some of his older siblings.

Doug got ringside tickets to the Tyler-Area Tough Man Competition in May—just in time for Mother's Day! Jennifer has never been an enthusiastic boxing fan, but agreed to accompany him to the fights provided she could bring along her needlework. She mostly wanted to make sure he didn't climb into the ring himself. The five oldest went with their dad to Doctors Camp this year, but David got sick without telling anyone the final night, and the scene to which Doug awoke Sunday morning made him wish they'd come home a day early…. The little boys were *pretending* one afternoon this month when Jennifer overheard Samuel tell his brothers, "Look! Here comes Daddy! He's walking on water!" This paints a fairly accurate picture of where Doug stands in Sam's estimation. His primary goal in life is to be exactly like his father—and he *already* has the obsessive/compulsive part down pat! Back in February, Jennifer found Sam's favorite T-shirt folded neatly around a pair of his blue jeans, socks, and underwear, all squirreled away in the corner of a remote bathroom cabinet. She made the mistake of moving these items back to his dresser drawers, only to send Samuel

into hysterics the following morning when he discovered them missing from their hiding place. He fervently explained that *that's the outfit he was planning to wear for his birthday* [8 months hence] *and he wanted to make sure it stayed clean for the occasion!*

We found out June 1 that #8 was on the way. Rumors to that effect had been floating around town since March, so it was nice to finally be able to confirm them. Doug spent two weeks and shed twenty pounds in El Paso with the Army Medical Reserves. It is the longest we've ever been separated. On our fourth night without him, Benjamin approached Mom with a furrowed brow and solemnly asked, "Is Daddy *dead*?" Doug immediately made arrangements to fly home for the weekend. He could stay only 16 hours, but it was enough to reassure Ben that his dad was still in the land of the living…. Jennifer's parents celebrated their 40th wedding anniversary on June 25. Unaware of the surprise reception their daughters had surreptitiously planned in their honor, they were astounded to find a roomful of family and friends where a secluded restaurant was supposed to have been. The event was an enormous success, although we ran out of punch cups toward the end of it. This, regrettably, did not faze the Flanders children, who found alternative means to slake their thirst (involving teaspoons and the punch fountain), thereby earning an A for resourcefulness, but an F for decorum. Jennifer conducted an intense review of the rules governing proper etiquette as soon as we got home.

Nana, Papa and Aunt Kimberly's family came to Tyler for the Fourth of July, boosting the attendance at our Independence Day block party to 55 this year. We went on another spring-cleaning rampage this month. Doug hired someone to help Jennifer paint the garage and landscape the backyard while he carted everything he could sneak past her to Goodwill. We received *unsolicited* help decluttering when hoodlums stole three of our bicycles in a span of two weeks! One bike was later returned after Sam spotted it at the swimming pool and Doug followed the rider home to discuss the matter with his parents. We got a new entertainment system to replace the TV we tossed out two years ago, but have avoided re-addiction, due largely to the fact that the equipment is so complicated, only Doug knows how to operate it. Meanwhile, we continue to read. We offered the children a quarter for every book report they wrote this summer, and they responded enthusiastically. Bethany led the pack as our top earner, while her brothers vied neck and neck for a not-too-distant second. We got our first taste of the controversial Harry Potter when Doug read *The Sorcerer's Stone* aloud this month, but the year's best read was *To Kill a Mockingbird*, despite our having to call the kids down periodically for playing "Boo Radley" after dark or quoting Scout's infamous lines at the dinner table whenever Mom serves ham…. The annual Cowan reunion was held July 29 at the aptly named *Funny Farm*. Some say our looniest members *married* into the family, but Doug actively *proved* the point by packing our suburban full of underage cousins after dinner and giving impromptu driving lessons in Uncle Jim's pasture!

Rebekah was walking by August, and David enjoyed the distinction of being the one to whom she toddled first. He spent half the summer dressed in buckskins, and Rebekah was the papoose he toted on his back. Lessons resumed mid-August, but the children still found time to hike through the woods and catch tadpoles in the creek. Jonathan and Bethany enjoyed longer excursions together, biking miles from home to browse through books at Barnes & Noble, snack on sandwiches at Jason's Deli, or admire animals at Petsmart. After spotting a particularly irresistible shepherd/collie pup, Jonathan emptied his bank account and brought the dog home. We named him Jinx, but with the exception of a few ill-placed puddles and an uprooted hydrangea, he's been no trouble at all…. In anticipation of our upcoming addition, we ordered a 15-passanger van, bought three trundle beds plus an 18-drawer chest, and shuffled room assignments. Ben, Joe and Rebekah now share the yellow bedroom, which received a facelift when we painted the lower walls green and added a botanical border this month; Sam and David moved in with Jon; and the crib in Bethany's room was reserved for the new baby. But all was for naught. Jennifer miscarried at 17 weeks—a perfectly formed baby boy, whom we named Joshua Adam. It made us so sad to lose him. When Doug brought Jennifer home from the hospital, the children consoled her with tearful hugs and kisses, homemade cards and bouquets, and the heartfelt pronouncement from David that (at least) "you still *look* pregnant, Mommy." This bittersweet reminder was fully intended to cheer Mom up, and strangely enough, it did.

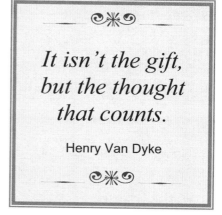

> *It isn't the gift, but the thought that counts.*
>
> Henry Van Dyke

Life marched on…. Jennifer and Bethany hosted their traditional Back-to-School Brunch in September, the same day Girlie-Girl celebrated her first birthday. Doug claims Rebekah looks more like her mother every day, but he's usually staring at her dimpled thighs when he says it! No longer does she perpetually smell of sour milk, having finally outgrown the exasperating habit of spitting up as she's lifted out of the bathtub, which had for 12 months been her knee-jerk reaction to smelling clean. We wrapped up a study of the American Revolution with a two-week tour of the East Coast, leaving town on Bethany's 11th birthday. We had scarcely driven out of Texas when Jennifer discovered the diamond was missing from her engagement ring—an irreplaceable heirloom that had been in Doug's family for generations. When our eagle-eyed David spotted it a week later amid cracker crumbs and crayons under the back seat, Doug dubbed him "Diamond Dave." Jonathan originally balked at the idea of dressing in Colonial garb to tour historic Williamsburg, as if doing so might embarrass him. (This, from the child who used to traipse all over Mesquite wearing mirrored goggles and a one-horned Viking helmet strapped to his head with a leather belt!) He really got in the spirit of things once Mom finished the costumes, though, and didn't want to take his off. We were stopped innumerable times by tourists who wanted to photograph or videotape our family. Curiously, this phenomenon continued even when we were in street clothes. Foreigners would indicate in broken English they wished us to line up, then would snap several pictures, presumably to show folks at home what a typical American family looks like. Rebekah didn't travel well this trip, due to a lingering ear infection and emerging molars. It's a good thing we had John Denver in the glove box. She didn't care for any other song on the CD, but would immediately stop crying, cock her head to one side, and grin from ear to ear every time we played (and replayed) "Thank God I'm a Country Boy!" We took Staten Island Ferry in New York to get a closer look at the Statue of Liberty. When we got caught in rush hour traffic afterwards, Jon and Beth reached under their seats, pulled out two scooters they'd smuggled from home, and coasted along the sidewalks of Manhattan next to our Suburban. We signed up for a four-hour whale-watching expedition while we were in Plymouth and were treated to magnificent views of several humpbacks. Doug and the children seemed unbothered by the wild rocking of our boat, but Jennifer was eventually forced below deck to be closer to the trashcan. There she developed a new appreciation for those long months the Pilgrims spent at sea. We found ourselves in Canada admiring Niagara Falls the day Samuel turned seven. In lieu of a birthday cake, Doug ordered snails, and with the exception of Jon and Ben, we all had our first (and probably last) taste of *escargot*.

We got home just in time for the Diabetes Walk in October. Jonathan raised $350 worth of donations in two days. Jennifer's sister waited until we were back in town to have her baby, so we got to meet Carolyn Cherree when she was only a day old. Having resigned ourselves to the fact we won't be needing that empty crib in Bethany's room any time soon, we took it apart and moved it to the attic. Two days later, we found out Jennifer is pregnant again—further proof that God delights in giving us the desires of our hearts! Bethany was selected as a semi-finalist in a poetry contest she entered this month. Her poem, entitled

"Daylight," will be published next year in the *Nature's Echo* anthology, but you can read it now by logging onto www.poetry.com.

By the first of November, our older children had assembled and distributed bundles of Bush/Cheney yard signs for the Republican Headquarters. Considering how these outnumbered area Gore signs 30 to 1, we never dreamed the election would be close, much less interminably disputed. Notwithstanding Gore's tireless and fraudulent attempts to manipulate numbers in his own favor, we are prayerfully awaiting Bush's long-overdue victory speech. Meanwhile, Doug has taken Jonathan and Bethany to Guatemala for a medical mission trip. Beth measured 5'7" when applying for her passport. (She was in tennis shoes at the time, but prefers her mother's heels, which now fit perfectly, as do most of the clothes in Jennifer's closet). At Doug's insistence, we learned Spanish before the trip and can carry on limited conversations *en Castellano* amongst ourselves, though it remains to be seen how they'll fare with native speakers. They'll be home December 2, provided none of Jonathan's hi-jacked-plane predictions materialize. To be on the safe side, Jon advised Nana to save the receipts for his Christmas gifts, so she can return them if he doesn't make it back.

And so ends another year. In a bustling household like ours, it's easy to become distracted by such futile objectives as keeping the laundry hamper *empty* or the pantry *full* (for more than a few fleeting minutes at a time)! December provides a great opportunity to shift our focus back where it belongs—upon our beautiful Lord and Savior, Jesus Christ, and upon the worthy goal of becoming more like Him. Just as important as *what* we do is the *attitude* with which we do it. We are quick to remind our children of this fact, but sometimes forget to apply it ourselves, as evidenced by the knot of wrinkles periodically stationed between our eyebrows. Laugh lines are far more attractive, which is reason enough to "rejoice in the Lord always, and in everything, give thanks." Won't you join us, as we commit anew to doing exactly that? We wish each of you a joyous and meaningful Christmas season and pray for you as for ourselves, that God's love may abound in our hearts, conforming us to the image of his blessed Son....

With love from the Flanders family:
Doug, Jennifer, Jonathan, Bethany, David, Samuel, Benjamin, Joseph & Rebekah

Greetings from Colonial Williamsburg

2001

Let me begin by noting that Doug, Jonathan, and Bethany did indeed make it home safely from Guatemala last December. They came laden with handcrafted souvenirs and brimming with animated accounts of their adventures abroad—climbing temple ruins in the jungles of Tikal, swimming in cascading pools formed by tropical volcanoes, and administering anesthesia with archaic equipment and no running water. When an ice storm blew through Tyler shortly after their return and knocked out our electricity for three days, we huddled under a pile of quilts and read *A Christmas Carol* by flashlight, the steam from our breath hanging in the air about us. The power was still out when Gore conceded the election, so we missed Bush's acceptance speech, after all. We received invitations to the inauguration, but were unwilling to pay $1000 a head to attend, much to the children's chagrin. Our new van arrived a few days before Christmas, looking more like a bus than a family car. All we need now is to have our school name painted down the side—something classic, like "**F**landers **A**cademy for **R**eally **T**alented **S**tudents."

Doug bought new bathroom scales in January, which are remarkable in that they also measure body fat percentage. For months afterward, he would drag them out any time we had company and subject our unsuspecting guests to surprise weight checks. Not everyone shared Doug's enthusiasm for new technology or his eagerness to compare vital statistics, but they dutifully followed the doctor's orders, removing their socks and shoes and stepping on the scales in turn. Rebekah learned to undress herself this month. She could squirm out of her shirt in a split second and would do so whenever/wherever the opportunity presented itself. The novelty of going topless did not wear off until spring, when she discovered her nostrils.

Bethany got braces in February. We found an orthodontist who gives sibling discounts, which means by the time we get to our last child, he should be paying us to straighten her teeth! Rebekah got tubes this month. She heard our dogs through closed windows the morning after her surgery, seemingly for the first time. This gives some indication of how badly compromised her hearing had been, since Jinx's barking wasn't easily ignored, as any of our sleep-deprived neighbors would readily attest. David turned nine.

Almost overnight, he progressed from perusing picture books to devouring 400-page novels! He also likes to climb trees, build forts, play ball, catch toads, and write pen pals. We traveled to Houston for a medical conference and brought Jennifer's parents along to help count heads. Even so, we managed one evening to leave Bethany in the ladies room of an Italian restaurant down the street from our hotel. As soon as she realized this was not just another of her dad's practical jokes, Beth had the maitre d' fax over a request for the Flanders to pick up their daughter posthaste. By the time we received it, however, we'd already discovered her absence and had dispatched Doug to retrieve her. "I tried to tell everyone we should wait for you," he teased, "but your mom said not to bother, since it was late and we needed to get to bed!" (Bethany knew better than to believe *that*!)

We drove to Washington-on-the-Brazos for Texas Independence Day. It began to pour rain almost as soon as we arrived. While the rest of us crowded under leaky canvas awnings

and watched re-enactors dig trenches around their tents, Doug negotiated a volume discount on lunch. He offered a vendor $10 for all the turkey legs she had left. She protested that they normally sell for $4 a piece, but Doug contended, between the growing storm and the diminishing crowd, that they wouldn't sell *at all* unless she accepted his offer—so she did! We continued our Texas history study back at home. We took square dancing lessons, attended a chili cook-off, and won a quilt raffle—all sponsored by our wonderful homeschool support group. The children had their portraits made this month, although it's becoming increasingly difficult to find a time when the whole crew looks simultaneously presentable. We had to postpone the first appointment after Joseph scribbled all over his brothers' extremities with a laundry marker one night while they were asleep. It took a week for the ink to wear off, by which time Rebekah had blisters under her nose from the undivided attention she'd been giving it lately. Meanwhile, Jon broke another finger playing basketball, and Joseph got run over by a bicycle. Although it left him completely *drenched* in blood, Joe's only injury was an inch-long gash to his forehead, which Dad sewed up at home under the sympathetic supervision of six siblings. The accident did little to slow Joseph down. Within days, he had persuaded Jonathan to take the training wheels off his bike and was riding easily without them. It was the *second* set of stitches that put him out of commission—three more in his foot two weeks later. That makes more stitches for Joe in a single month than the rest of our kids have had in their entire lives combined! But what can you expect from a child whose birthday is 9/11?

Jonathan saved a baby squirrel from a couple of cats in April and nursed it back to health. The grateful creature later returned the favor by dragging our spank-stick so far up a tree that Mom couldn't reach it! David rescued the spring pigeons that fell down our flue this year. *Flash* was ready to fly and didn't tarry, but *Smokey* lingered in the ligustrum for weeks, next to a family of sparrows living in our wren house. Rebekah found a new obsession this month—she learned how to *wink*. Her constant practice made us fear she'd developed an involuntary twitch, but we eventually realized she was doing it on purpose. We had a memorable Easter weekend: Doug involved our van in a 3-car fender-bender, David hurled a baseball through our dining room window, Joe chipped two teeth and knocked three loose, and our "resurrection cookies" didn't *rise*. They looked more like flat pancakes than hollow tombs, but the *original* grave was empty, and that's what *matters*! Spring-cleaning yielded longer lasting results than usual this year, since we began charging the children for everything they leave out of place. The little boys caught on while the going price was

Christmas is not as much about opening our presents as opening our hearts.

Janice Maeditere

a nickel an item, but we had to up the ante several times before Jonathan mended his ways. Doug and Jennifer got matching watches to celebrate the anniversary of the day they met, 15 years ago this month. We drove to San Antonio, stopping in Austin to tour the capital and watch the colony of 1.5 million bats come out from under Congress Avenue Bridge. We found a nice, green knoll shortly before dusk and sat down to wait, but by the time the bats emerged—*three hours later*—it was too dark to see them at all, though we could hear their cries and feel occasional droppings as they passed overhead. Ughh! We had better success with winged creatures on the Riverwalk. The birds there have apparently developed a taste for tortilla chips, and our children were more than happy to share with the huge flock that assembled around our table at Casa Rio. Rain accompanied us on *this* Texas fieldtrip, too, causing the Fiesta River Parade to be cancelled for the first time in sixty years! Doug didn't let this dampen *his* spirits, but took advantage of the wet weather to do some power shopping, which naturally included the purchase of more athletic shoes....

In May, we attended a homeschool book fair in Arlington, but were forced to cut our stay short when two of the children got sick. Within days, all seven were ill. Presenting symptoms were commonplace enough—sore throats, nausea and vomiting—but by the time the bug had run its course, the kids were clutching their heads and howling hysterically, as if they had beetles in their brains. Between outbursts, we read aloud. Mom *finished Robinson Crusoe* and *Carry On, Mr. Bowditch* in the afternoons, while Dad regaled us with *Cheaper by the Dozen* and *Belles on their Toes* during the evening hours. Jonathan had a birthday and

officially entered his *teen* years. If he can manage to finish this stage of life with as sweet an attitude as he's begun it, we'll be in great shape. He volunteered at the hospital all summer, having become particularly interested in emergency medicine. He never goes *anywhere* without a well-stocked first-aid kit, which is fortuitous, considering *Joseph* seldom goes anywhere without needing one! Jonathan served as sort of a "poster-child" for Juvenile Diabetes this summer when two different television stations interviewed him for their evening newscasts. He even starred in a commercial advertising the annual Diabetes Walk at Bergfeld Park; it was only a 30-second spot, but it took about three hours to film!

By June, the so-called *German shepherd* pup that Jonathan adopted last fall had grown into a wooly mammoth *Chow*, with a temperament to match. Our little ones could no longer venture into the backyard without being nosed, nipped or knocked to the ground. Fearing Jinx might do to the children what he'd done to our gardenias, Doug wasted no time in returning the dog to the Humane Society. We looked at a spec-home in Brighton Creek this month, and word spread like wildfire. We were subsequently flooded with phone calls from builders, bankers, and real-estate brokers convinced we were ready to buy some million-dollar mansion, but we opted to keep our own modest home (with its modest mortgage) and just re-carpet, instead. With baby's due date more imminent than we imagined, Doug left town for a two-week stint with the Army Reserves, and Jennifer's nesting instinct kicked into overdrive. Even as hubby was repelling off 50-foot towers and experiencing first-hand the effects of tear gas, Jennifer was carting home truckloads of cleaning, painting, gardening, plumbing, and electrical supplies, determined to refurbish our entire estate before Doug returned. Unfortunately, a reprise of last month's *screaming virus* thwarted her progress; she stayed so busy laundering bed linens and meting out Motrin that the other projects were barely begun before Dad was due back. He arrived to find the house completely uninhabitable: furniture stacked to the ceiling, gaping holes where toilets should be, landscaping limp from lack of water, epoxy fumes permeating every room, and the family checked into a hotel, waiting for the air to clear. Such was the state of affairs when Jennifer's labor began—two weeks early and exactly eight hours after Doug's plane touched down! We were blessed with another beautiful baby girl, Rachel Joy, born June 16. She weighed 8 lbs 8 oz, our smallest yet, and Doug immediately took to calling her "Peanut." Rebekah calls her *MY* baby, and firmly believes it's true. While Jennifer was in the hospital, Nana and Papa watched our kids and supervised the carpet-laying, toilet-resetting, furniture-placement, etc. They undoubtedly returned home with a more acute appreciation for their own quiet, orderly, empty nest.

July was largely uneventful. Jennifer nursed round the clock. Doug *ran* a lot, still hoping to be ready for his first marathon sometime before rigor mortis sets in. Jonathan *lived* at the medical center. Bethany baked bookoos of bread. The middle boys spent their waking hours on their bikes or at the pool. Samuel taught Joseph how to swim and do flips off the diving board this summer—Joe landed *in the water* all but once. Sensing we were about to embark on another cross-country trip, Rebekah became suddenly intent on potty training. Twice, Jennifer caught her naked in the dog run, squatting over Lucky's water bowl! Given this eager enthusiasm and her insatiable passion for flushing things down the toilet, we thought it best to cooperate, though we didn't relish the idea of stopping at every gas station she spotted between here and Yellowstone.

August took us on a 10-state tour of the Midwest. Our first stop was Branson, MO, where our 11 p.m. arrival inadvertently landed us smack in the middle of a hot rod parade! Spectators pointed, laughed, and cheered as our van inched its way down Main Street—clearly out of place amid the sea of sports cars. We felt a strong urge to toss candy out the windows and set our tires spinning, but resisted. The procession delayed us two hours and cost us our hotel reservation, since the front desk was closed by the time we reached our destination. We had to scramble to find a vacancy elsewhere. Packing ten people into a single room may sound cramped, but it beats camping-out on the parking lot, and promotes *togetherness*, besides! And how else would we have discovered that *David* talks in his sleep, had we not been there to hear him cry out, "Dear God! Please *help* me!"

> To perceive Christmas through its wrapping becomes more difficult with every year.
>
> E.B. White

when he had a nightmare? (We were glad to learn that *prayer* is his instinctive response to trouble). We shopped the 78-acre Mall of America in Minneapolis, MN, where Doug astounded us all by *not buying a thing* (he made up for it later in Native American pottery purchases)! The children panned for gold in Lead, SD, but Dad dug for treasure of a different sort, pulling an eight-inch strand of cheese from Joseph's throat when he tried to choke to death on some fried mozzarella. We skipped stones on the Shoshone River and scaled cliffs in the Badlands, two impromptu but unforgettable wayside stops. The Air Force Academy in Colorado Springs certainly made a big impression—*Joseph* didn't want to leave. The mountain air must have agreed with Rachel; she'd grown an inch longer and a pound heavier by the time we got home. She was much too big to sleep in the laundry basket any longer, so we moved her to a crib.

September signaled the beginning of birthday season. Rebekah celebrated her second. It's hard to believe this chunky monkey *ever* had trouble gaining weight! She'll swallow anything she can get her hands on, believing unlocked pantries or overflowing trashcans to be open invitations to "dig in." She loves books, although up until recently, she has insisted on turning all the pages herself and would seldom slow down long enough for anyone to actually *read the text*. September 11 arrived, and while tragic news of hi-jacked planes and suicide bombings gripped worldwide attention, Joseph quietly turned four. *Purple* is Joe's favorite color, and his favorite pastimes include raiding the candy dish at Mr. and Mrs. Brown's house, watching *Bambi*, offering lengthy prayers at the dinner table that God alone can understand, and giving the sort of strong, vigorous kisses one might expect to receive from a leech. He *sure* loves his family, and he *sure* tells us often! Bethany is now twelve, going on twenty. She continues to read widely, is an accomplished artist, prolific writer, talented musician, experienced babysitter, and terrific cook. We went to Six Flags for Beth's birthday, realizing too late that the rest of the crowd was there to celebrate Something Else. It was "a van among sports cars" all over again as our family-of-ten warily wormed its way through a park full of [mostly male] couples who were swaying arm-in-arm as they sang along with a live performance of *Stand by Your Man*!

Samuel had his eighth birthday in October. A born mathematician, he is constantly engaged in *some* sort of mental calculation—how many minutes constitute a four-day visit to Nana and Papa's, how big a slice of pie would result if he halved a piece six times, how much spending money would be left after tithes and taxes were our family to win 50 million dollars and split it nine ways! He adores his father and refuses to get dressed until he knows what Doug is wearing, so that they can *match*. All he wanted for his birthday this year was *a day alone with dad*, every minute of which Sam planned a month in advance and reviewed ten times daily with anyone who'd listen. Benjamin turned six this month. He has made tremendous strides in speech therapy and continues to participate in gymnastics and choir. He's an eager student, a dependable errand-boy, an enthusiastic baby-cuddler, and a borderline vegetarian, subsisting almost entirely on peanut butter sandwiches (no jelly), raw broccoli, cheese pizza, and cream gravy.

Rebekah must have thought she'd died and gone to heaven November 1 when she crept out of bed in the wee hours of the morning to find a house full of Halloween candy, unattended! By the time our 5 a.m. alarm sounded, all that was left was wall-to-wall wrappers! Doug and the middle boys attended a father/son retreat at Pine Cove and came home addicted to "four-square." Even before their bags were unpacked, they were outside taping a court onto our driveway, so they could teach the rest of the family how to play. Soon, every boy in the neighborhood was lining up with us to compete in an ongoing, afterschool tournament. Bethany made her acting debut this month, playing the *older sister* of a 16-year old Anne in Tyler Civic Theater's fall production of *The Diary of Anne Frank*. She handled the part beautifully. David appeared in one act, as well, albeit unintentionally, when his ill-timed parting of the theater curtains provided an unsolicited stand-in for a Nazi soldier. He got *rave* reviews.

December promises to be busy, but bright. We'll bid *adieu* to a few more Flanders tonsils this month—both Joe and Rebekah are scheduled to have theirs removed on the December 19. Rachel, who has endured three ear infections in four months, may join them for tubes. I'm low on space, so I'll close by wishing you a "Merry Christmas and Happy New Year!" Let us hear from you soon!

With love from the Flanders family:
Doug, Jennifer, Jonathan, Bethany, David, Samuel, Benjamin, Joseph, Rebekah & Rachel

Holiday Parties for Children

For many years when our kids were little, we invited all the neighborhood children over in December for a "Birthday Party for Jesus." We'd play "Put the Baby in the Manger" (as opposed to "Pin the Tail on the Donkey") and break open a star-shaped piñata (after following it all around the house like wise men). Jennifer would read the Christmas story aloud while the kids worked on related coloring pages, and then we'd dress up in oversized T-shirts and fabric scarves (gold lame' for angels, muslin or wool for shepherds) and act out the story.

As our kids got older, we eventually replaced the neighborhood birthday party with a "Shoebox Stuffing Party." All the guests bring goodies to put in boxes for Operation Christmas Child, and we all wrap and stuff the boxes together. Since most of the children who will receive our boxes live in countries where rice and beans are staple foods, that's what we serve for dinner at the party. Once the boxes are filled, we gather around them and pray for the kids who will be receiving our gifts. This is a great service project for the whole family.

2002

The children's surgeries went well last December. Joseph relinquished his tonsils and Rebekah her adenoids without complaint, and both felt chipper enough to sit through an opening-day matinee of the long-awaited *Lord of the Rings* that same afternoon.

Doug attended a medical conference in January aboard the world's largest cruise ship, *Voyager of the Seas*, and took the family along for the ride. Granted, our cabins were the size of a walk-in closet, but the beds were comfortable, and the scopolamine patches we'd packed for seasickness helped with claustrophobia, as well. Besides, the close quarters provided a captive audience for David and Samuel, who roomed with Nana and Papa and staged nightly recitals on the bamboo violins they'd bought in the marketplace. High points of this vacation included climbing Dunn's River Falls in Jamaica, swimming with stingrays off the Cayman Islands, and snorkeling in Cozumel. The low points were eating an interminably interrupted lunch along the way at a certain restaurant/gift shop (the name of which Doug has since forbidden the children to ever even *mention* again) and getting locked out of our van, thirty miles from port, half an hour before boarding time (thanks a lot, Mom)—even Jonathan's *Worst-Case Scenario Survival Handbook* couldn't get us out of *that* fix. A Caribbean plantation worker showed our children how to scale coconut palms using a small, circular climbing rope; thereafter, every time we turned around, all five boys had scampered up the trunk of another tree and disappeared into the foliage overhead. We took several snapshots of them swinging from the branches like so many chimpanzees. These were about the only pictures we got of *Joseph* on this trip, as he turned camera-shy after the ship photographer showed up at dinner one night dressed in a pirate costume and brandishing a machete. Of course, the cruise cuisine was fabulous. No telling how much weight Doug and Jennifer would have gained had the food on *their* plates not appealed so much more to Rebekah than anything on her *own*. Rachel never found her sea legs, though it wasn't for lack of trying. She spent floor time propped on hands and *toes*, and had learned to crawl by the time we disembarked. Jennifer gave us a scare on the drive home when she was suddenly struck blind in one eye. Her left pupil had blown to the size of a marble, and we were guessing intracranial bleed? Doug was en route to the nearest hospital before we made a connection between the rapid onset of this malady and the removal of her scopolamine patch. She must have rubbed some residue in her eye and caused it to dilate, a freakish condition that lasted 24 hours!

February brought restored order to our happy household, although Jennifer suspects it had less to do with our new school schedule than it did with Nana's prayers—undoubtedly more *specific* after our concentrated time together on that cruise! David turned 10 this month and was promoted from trash collecting to laundry duty. He now processes 20 loads a week competently and cheerfully. His free time is spent reading books, playing tennis, and practicing piano (when he first began lessons, he couldn't pass a piano without sitting down to play, but that early enthusiasm has waned somewhat). Rachel began solids. She's not overly fond of baby food, but can swallow her weight in refried beans and guacamole. Doug achieved his life-long goal of completing a marathon, and Jennifer was behind him every step of the way—*literally!* Eternal optimist that he is, Doug convinced her that the past 14 years of childbearing counted as "surreptitious training" and put her in prime cardiovascular condition (never mind the fact that when we started, she could scarcely trot ten yards without getting winded); so after an additional Six Months of Rigorous Training (not including January), we packed up our *PowerBars* and headed to Austin. I don't imagine what we were doing could properly be called *running*—it was more of a 20-mile jog plus a 6-mile cool down—but we nevertheless managed to cross the finish line, hand-in-hand, *before* they stopped the clock!

March found us scouring every thrift store in town for camouflage clothing, trying to piece together enough battle dress uniforms to send our boys to boot camp. Watching these thirty would-be soldiers in the field with their dads—running obstacle courses, digging foxholes, practicing marksmanship, and choking down ready-to-eat rations—one might think they'd joined a militia, but it was actually a hands-on history lesson, part of the WWII study our homeschool group sponsored this spring. Lest the boys have all the fun, Jennifer took Bethany and the nursing baby to Jefferson the following weekend for three tranquil days of shopping, scrapbooking, and sightseeing in *The Bed & Breakfast Capitol of the World*…. Whenever the kids work our house into an especial state of disorder, we say it looks like a tornado struck it, but in March one nearly *did*. It sucked the windows clean out of our cars and about did the same to our eardrums. The accompanying power outage sent us scurrying for flashlights and gathering babies, but it wasn't until we later ventured outdoors that we realized how close we'd come to meeting our Maker. Uprooted trees surrounded our house like a ring of toppled dominoes, but by God's mercy, they all fell clear of *us*!

April took Doug to New Orleans for another medical conference, with Jonathan in tow. The two spent mornings listening to trauma lectures, afternoons absorbing the sights and sounds of Jazzfest, and evenings dining in five-star restaurants. The rest of us stayed at home and (*finally!*) polished off the last of our Y2K provisions. I doubt the children will *ever* be as fond of sugarcoated cereals as they were before we purchased all those cases of Froot Loops off the clearance rack!

Doug drove to Houston in May for yet another conference. David tagged along this trip and learned to intubate a rubber dummy while Dad practiced the same fiber-optic procedure on fully conscious volunteers. There was enough time between workshops to visit the zoo, go paddle boating, and take in the new *Spiderman* movie…. Jennifer's mother shared her best household hints with our homeschool moms this month; her cleaning tips came in handy the following week when Joseph slid a penny behind his nightlight, melted the coin, shorted the circuit, and burned a black blotch on the bedroom wall. It is a wonder he was not electrocuted. God must have extraordinary plans for Joe's life, as often as it has been spared his first five years. We played some baseball this spring. Despite the aforementioned accident-proneness, our children are nowhere near as clumsy as Doug feared they'd be when he first took note of Jennifer tripping across campus at DBU back in 1986! On the contrary, they all have superb hand-eye coordination—and surprisingly strong throwing arms, as we learned when the police department stationed one of those computerized speedometers at the end of our driveway: it not only slowed traffic around

our corner, but allowed us to clock the velocity of our fast balls (try as we might, none of us could beat the neighbor boy's 62 mph pitches)…. Ben lost his first tooth. Ever cautious, he insisted Mom *pull* it as soon as it started to wiggle, to avoid choking on it later (this was no easy task, as the tooth was small, slippery, and only slightly loose). Jonathan turned 14 this month and informed us he'd adopted a new motto: "*If you want to be first in the kingdom of heaven, you've got to be servant of all*" (which is a dramatic improvement over "*It's easier to ask forgiveness than permission!*"). He put the platitude to good practice by volunteering at ETMC again this summer, as well as donating time to the Red Cross and to the American Diabetes Association. His other interests include whittling hiking sticks, playing the guitar, studying *Wilderness Medicine*, memorizing the New Testament (2 books down, 25 to go), and earning money for the Jeep he hopes to buy when he turns 16.

We participated in the Mesquite Rodeo Bike Ride in June. Jennifer trailed the younger children on the 10-mile course, while Doug and Jonathan used the 20-mile route to break in new triathlon cycles. Still too young to candy-stripe at the hospital with Jon, Bethany began volunteering at Green Acres Library, where she helped organize the summer reading program and led a weekly story time for preschoolers. Rachel celebrated her first birthday on Father's Day. She has a mouthful of teeth, but seldom flashes her sweet smile in public, being more apt to show strangers (especially photographers) a well-practiced poker face, instead, or a wrinkled-nose expression that seems to protest, "What is that *horrid smell?*" She has learned to clap her hands, wave bye-bye, stand alone, and play peek-a-boo. The amazing thing is not that she's developing right on schedule, but that each new milestone brings such unmitigated delight to the rest of the family, even the eighth time around! Of course, we couldn't let *spring* slip by without tackling some huge home-improvement project, so Doug arranged to have the interior of our house repainted this year. To get an idea of what life was like during the twelve days it took to achieve that end, simply push all the furniture to the middle of your house, heap the contents of every closet, cupboard, and drawer on top of that, coat the surrounding walls with latex, drop a passel of youngsters in the middle of the mess, and do what you can to ensure they don't touch the paint, topple the piles, or track the drips! Our painters must've thought we were *muy loco* to expect them to work with *ochos niños* underfoot. They persevered good-naturedly, but we were *all* smiling when the job was done!

Rebekah figured out how to disconnect the hose to our super-capacity washing machine in July. It's amazing how far seven cubic feet of water will go! It took six days to refinish the floors, but this time we just left the contractor a house key and spent the week at Pine Cove in Crier Creek. Family camp was great, though it wrecked the five-hour-per-day reading streak Samuel and David had maintained through the month of June (too many distractions). Upon our return home, Jennifer and Bethany began the Body-for-LIFE program, having been duly inspired by all the before/after photos plastered across the cover of Bill Philip's bestseller. The girls found weight training less distasteful than distance running—they shed unwanted pounds, but got to *keep* their toenails!

By August, Rachel was walking and beginning to pair such words as, *"Hey, ya'll!"* (spoken like a true Texan). Doug brought home a black Hummer2 this month, demonstrating once again the truth of that old adage concerning the difference between men and boys. The kids pitched a tent in our backyard and camped-out for a week before school started, trying to pack as much fun as possible into the last few days of summer vacation. All too soon, Mom set them back to their lessons, heartless taskmaster that she is.

Rebekah turned three in September. Jon bought a box of cartoon Band-aids to use in bandaging her scrapes (she gets plenty trying to keep up with her brothers), but now she cries hysterically, *"I need Scooby Doo!"* at the slightest bump or bruise. We've had to switch back to the plain, flesh-colored variety to curb her hypochondria! Rebekah loves to make up songs, paint her nails, and express contrary viewpoints (just try to convince her that *grass is green* or that *she's a person*). She can be a mite stubborn, but we love her anyway and never tire of hearing her confess, "I luh boo, too!" Joseph turned five this month. He enjoys cutting paper, sorting socks, digging holes, and playing *Boggle Jr*. He also likes to color and can stay inside the lines remarkably well, although doing so demands his full concentration and an inordinate amount of *tongue* action. Our multi-talented Bethany had her birthday this month, adding a *second* teenager to our household equation! Despite the attendant hormonal fluctuations, we are thoroughly enjoying this new stage of our children's lives. It is gratifying to watch them grow in wisdom and maturity, as they stand on the very brink of adulthood. They're terrific kids, in our unabashedly biased opinion!

October was a banner month for Doug: he was elected president of his anesthesia group, soon to be 43 physicians strong, and was promoted to major in the Army Medical Reserves, effective June 2000. On the down side, he also received special recognition from the Texas Department of Public Safety for having paid enough uncontested speeding tickets over the past couple of years to warrant a brief suspension of his driver's license. Ouch! Samuel turned nine this month. Our most enthusiastic fan of Mom's home cooking, he has a voracious appetite for *knowledge*, as well. Sam told us last spring that he reckons himself "one of the hundred smartest 8-year olds in the world" (he's certainly one of the hundred most *confident*)! For fun, he and David like to search the dictionary for unusual words and then quiz one another on their meanings (this game, like countless others, eventually devolves into a no-holds-barred wrestling match, executed with the raucous gusto that will drive a mother crazy). Ben-Ben celebrated his seventh birthday. When he's not pouring over our *Childcraft Encyclopedias*, he likes to cuddle the baby, study maps, eat popsicles, and work jigsaw puzzles. He officially began first grade this fall, but his *favorite* subject is "craft time" with Bethany, the fruits from which are invariably dedicated to Mom, with love.

We traveled to Oklahoma for the Nobles family reunion in November and enjoyed some fabulous fall foliage on our drive through Mena. This was the first time we'd seen some of Jennifer's relatives in about eight years, so it's nice that Joseph and Rebekah, partners-in-crime, waited until we *got home* to chop off one another's hair(!). We spent much of this autumn immersed in the Middle Ages, this semester's historical topic for our home school support group. We studied the Crusades, took sword-fighting lessons, made paper, learned the art of chainmail, sang Gregorian chants, designed a family coat-of-arms, and read *The Canterbury Tales* (though not in Anglo Saxon). We even drove to Plantersville to attend the Texas Renaissance Festival. We opted against wearing our woolen costumes since the day was unseasonably warm, but we counted several scantily clad belly dancers parading around the fair grounds for whom the heat must have been a welcome respite.

Thus the year flew swiftly by. God willing, we'll spend the holidays in Branson this year with both sets of parents, our sisters, and their families. Perhaps we'll even see that White Christmas of which we've so often sung. Benjamin is praying for "a *LONG* winter… maybe even *two weeks!*" Doug and Jennifer are hoping for a mild one, as we are scheduled to begin building a new house in January and hope to finish before school resumes next fall. Add to that little project the fact that we have another baby due in May, and you have the recipe for a very full year! Pray that God gives us grace to meet all the challenges inherent in such endeavors. We pray, likewise, that 2003 will see *you* grow closer to our glorious Lord and Savior, Jesus Christ, and that He may be honored in everything you do. Let us hear from you soon!

With love from the Flanders family:
Doug and Jennifer, Jonathan, Bethany, David, Samuel,
Benjamin, Joseph, Rebekah, Rachel and Baby-Boo

Photo by W.H. Cowan

2003

The mind of man plans his way, but the LORD directs his steps (Proverbs 16:9). As if building a house, having a baby, and taking over the ETAA presidency did not promise *enough* excitement for the coming year, Doug received word last December that his Army Reserve unit was being activated. He was told to pack up his gear and await further instructions concerning when and where to report. Thus began what Kurt Vonnegut would call our "dancing lessons from God." We spent Christmas in Missouri, as planned, although illness kept Doug's parents from joining us. The rest of the family had a terrific time trudging around Big Cedar Lodge in 14 inches of fresh-fallen snow and roasting marshmallows over the blazing fires the boys kept burning in our cabins.

Pressures mounted in January when we were selected for a random audit by the IRS. They primarily wanted proof that all of our children actually *exist*, though I don't see why it should matter, since we are no longer allowed to *deduct* any of them! Of course, we *are* allowed to deduct such things as Doug's portion of travel expenses incurred while attending medical conferences, but when Jennifer began bragging to the tax adjuster what a great deal that gave us on last year's cruise, Doug thought it inappropriate and issued a swift kick under the table to silence her. When he later tried to apologize, she laughed, "You didn't kick *ME*!" Fortunately, a bruised shin was not enough to keep our amicable auditor from filing the first "No Change" he'd had in years. The Army piled on paperwork when Doug's security clearance had to be renewed this month, forcing him to track down everything from "college roommate's current address" to "last job's supervisor's middle name." The anesthesia presidency also proved more time-consuming than anticipated. We felt desperate to get away from phones and faxes, but were so dog-tired by the time Doug got a long weekend that we opted to stay at home and watch a documentary on *The 50 Years War* instead. How's *that* for an exotic vacation?

We forged ahead with our building plans in February. Once the trees were cleared to make room for it, our house seemed a lot bigger than it looked on paper! The land developer joked with passers-by that a new private school was being built on the lot. It is nestled on two wooded acres and surrounded by hiking trails that beckon our children to come explore the little lake that lies at the foot of the hill. Thus they spent many glad hours this summer, while Mom and Dad surveyed the slow but steady progress being made on our new home…. Bethany learned to cut hair this month, thanks to her brothers' willingness to serve as guinea pigs. Inspired, Rebekah did a little hairstyling of her own. She brushed the tangles from Mom's waist-length tresses, then retrieved what Jennifer assumed was a barrette when she felt its cold, metallic edge slide against the crown of her head. Blessings be upon our observant Sam, who snatched the scissors from sister's hands and spared his unsuspecting mother a severe scalping! Undaunted, Bekah simply smuggled the scissors into bed at naptime, where she buzzed two Barbies and gave herself a mullet, unhindered.

Doug received orders on the Ides of March to report at once to Fort Sam Houston, *a copy of his will in hand*! That was hardly reassuring, but as Providence would have it, he spent his entire 90-day "tour of duty" stationed in San Antonio, administering anesthesia at Brook Army Medical Center, but ready to defend the Alamo should the need arise. He was still driving that Hummer2 (and would routinely take Jennifer *garage-saling* in it, although doing so severely diminished her ability to negotiate lower prices!). This has become one of the hottest-selling cars in America right now, despite attempts by various environmental groups to blackball the gas-guzzler. When told of an anti-Hummer billboard campaign that inquires of passing motorists, "What would *Jesus* drive?", Doug argued in favor of the H2: "After all," he reasoned, "it's just a modern-day donkey. *Both come equipped with heated leather seats and are great for going off-road.*" But he has since repented and is back in a truck…. Bethany served as an Azalea Belle this month. Donning an antebellum dress, she stood on the lawns of Tyler's historic homes and greeted visitors during the three weekends the azaleas were in bloom. It took some major alterations to get her hoop skirt and ball gown to fit again—at six foot, she's 13 inches taller than *last* time she wore it. The boys pulled their old Confederate uniforms out of storage, as well, to reenact a few battles at a friend's "Civil War" birthday party. Their pretend skirmishes came days after Mom had scheduled school time for our five oldest to see the newly released *Gods and Generals* at the theater. This film made a lasting impression. Our daring David, now 11, was especially moved by Stonewall Jackson's belief that the sovereignty of God kept him "as safe on the battlefield as [he was] in bed." Jennifer was quick to balance this conviction (which we whole-heartedly share) with an observation that the courageous general did not abandon *all* caution, and neither should he.

Our home school group wrapped up a yearlong study of the Middle Ages in April with an extravagant feast and three-hour play. Jon was a monk, Bethany a lady-in-waiting, David a court jester (a role for which he was definitely typecast!), Samuel head page, and Ben a chorus member. Little Rachel made her acting debut a week earlier, sharing the stage with David and Bethany in *A Midsummer Night's Dream*. With blonde locks and rosy cheeks, she made an unlikely "Indian boy," but played a convincing baby. We spent the rest of the month in San Antonio with Doug, who had by that time moved to an apartment off base. It had two bedrooms (three, if you count the master closet which doubled as a nursery; four, if you include the storage space under the stairs which Joe enthusiastically claimed for his own) and one very easily overwhelmed toilet, but for all the *indoors* lacked in space and fresh air, the *outdoors* more than compensated. The apartment grounds boasted three separate pools, a beautiful tree-lined lake, and a mile-long jogging trail that looped behind the local library. The children raced through their studies every morning and spent afternoons hiking, swimming, fishing, feeding ducks, and browsing bookshelves. It was a nice change of pace.

Roses are reddish
Violets are blueish
If it weren't for
Christmas
We'd all be Jewish

Benny Hill

Jonathan turned 15 in May, completed Driver's Ed and got his learner's permit. The hardship of having a mother who can't stay awake on the road gave him plenty of driving experience on our frequent trips to San Antonio. We're proud of how responsible and conscientious Jon is behind the wheel. We also think that anyone who must learn to drive (*and* parallel park!) in a loaded, 15-passenger van deserves some sort of medal! Mom taught him early to make sure she'd have a ride to the hospital, should Dad and all the neighbors be simultaneously away from home when she went into labor. As it happened, Doug was on hand to escort Jennifer to the maternity ward through TWO false alarms—you'd think a woman who's already given birth *eight times over* would know the difference between breaking her water and wetting her pants, but such is evidently not the case! Doug was still miles from home, however, when Jennifer was admitted for a last-minute induction on her due date, but made it to her bedside a good *three hours* before the baby arrived. Isaac Edward was born on May 22, a healthy 9 lbs 6 oz and 22½ inches. He's absolutely beautiful (Dad says he got a triple-coat of *pretty*-paint), and he's been happy from the get-go, so the name suits him well. Although our boys now outnumber the girls 2-to-1, we've heard no complaints over the disproportionate ratio (there's nothing like having a couple of little sisters to make Bethany better appreciate her brothers, who've never shown the slightest interest in that stash of lip gloss and nail polish which so entices Rachel and Rebekah). Even Joe, who'd voiced a hope that Mom would bring a *puppy* home from the hospital, was in nowise disappointed.

Rebekah's curiosity got the best of her when the boys brought a red-eared slider home from the creek in June. Having grown weary of her attempts to coax him from his shell, the turtle latched onto her finger and refused to let go. The bite did no real damage, although her cries of distress would've convinced anyone within earshot that she'd been mortally wounded. Prying the creature's jaws open was a simple matter of finding the right-sized screwdriver; unfortunately for Rebekah, it took ten minutes of head-scratching and failed-other-attempts for us to come up with that solution…. Rachel Joy turned two this month. Our gentle little lamb certainly lives up to her name: she spreads smiles and sunshine wherever she goes. Her siblings used to squabble over who'd be first to play with her when she wakes up, until the middle boys began dividing the morning into half-hour increments, setting a timer, and taking turns. One day, Ben claimed the 7:30-8:00 a.m. time slot, but was precisely two minutes late handing Rachel off to the next in line. Samuel arbitrated, "That means *I* get her until 8:34, then *David* can have her until 9:06!" They try to out-do one another entertaining her— galloping through the house with Rachel on their backs, pulling her across the brick floors on a quilt sling, or taking her outside to swing and pick posies. Happy regardless, she never grows weary of their attention…. Doug finished his three months with the Army (hooray!), and we celebrated with a trip to Sea World (they were offering free admission to active-duty soldiers and their families—an *incredible* deal for *us!*). We swung through Gruene on our way back to Tyler. While Dad accompanied the four oldest on a six-mile tubing expedition down the more-treacherous-than-it-looks Guadalupe River, Mom took our five youngest *antiquing*—which should qualify as an extreme sport in its own right!

We had a terrific time at Crier Creek's Family Camp again this July. Jonathan won a "First Aid Award" for the care he rendered wounded campers throughout the week. Jennifer was given the "Shopping Award," having returned from a field trip to nearby Columbus with six antique bar stools and a nearly-life-sized statue of three children on a slide. Doug would have earned a "Packing Award" had one existed, for managing to fit these purchases into our 15-passenger van for the drive home—along with five mountain bikes, three suitcases, six backpacks, two diaper bags, three car seats, 11 people, and a jogging stroller!

We cast the family's footprints in wet cement when the driveway for our new house was poured in August. Jennifer's parents were here to witness this event, but the thought of how such an act might affect our home's resale value was almost more than Nana could bear. Summer vacation ended, and we started back to school. Lessons at home were augmented this year with Tuesday morning classes at Cottage Garden in Spanish, sign language, science, art, and Greek mythology. Rebekah finally learned to wipe her bottom this month, which was cause for great rejoicing among those of us who had been doing the job for her. She'd hitherto refused to even attempt the task herself, presumably to guard against germs, although no such thought ever stopped her from *gleaning used chewing gum* from underneath restaurant tables or stepping on stray gummy bears (so Mom won't see her pick them off the ground), then *licking them off the bottom of her shoe* when she thinks nobody's watching!

We attended Jennifer's 20-year high school reunion in September. Bringing Isaac along made her feel a bit like the baby-toting hick from *Sweet Home Alabama*, but what else *can* you do with a nursing infant who won't take a bottle, save keep him close to Mama? Rebekah turned four this month. She can be surprisingly headstrong, an inherited trait that repeatedly drives Doug and Jennifer to our knees (as well as to the woodshed!) and makes us more deeply appreciate what our *own* parents endured raising *us*. Rebekah loves to talk, full-volume, non-stop, sun-up to sun-down, and anyone who dares squeeze a word in edge-wise is met with an indignant rebuke: "You are GOOFING UP my STORY!" (or worse, "Stop saying 'BE QUIET'—that's getting on my NERVES!"). Much of our child-training energy has been directed at helping this precocious little chatterbox develop a measure of self-control in how, when, and to what length she expresses herself! Joseph, who prefers to be called *Rob* for reasons beyond our comprehension, celebrated his sixth birthday this month. Despite having occasional panic attacks over the thought that *his tonsils might grow back*, he remains fairly laid-back and easy-going. He's the self-appointed doorman to half of Tyler—visit whichever restaurant lets kids eat free on any given night of the week and you'll likely find him manning the entrance, holding doors open for fellow diners.... Bethany spent several days with her grandparents after turning 14. Nana pampered her with manicures, pedicures, and trips to the mall, where they shopped 'til they dropped. Beth's learned to make soap, can tomatoes, quilt, and crochet, but her most *life-changing* accomplishment this year may have been breaking her parents' rickety old four-poster while demonstrating some powerhouse karate moves. The replacement mattress, box springs, and frame have been so much more comfortable (and quiet) than the old ones that we almost wish she'd sparred with the bed years ago.

Samuel turned 10 in October. He always has a ready smile. Having been assigned to KP all year, Sam cleaned up after every meal with nary a complaint. It's a fitting assignment, as he and brothers David and Jon do more cooking than anyone else in the family. All three have hollow legs. Mom once brought a carton of 2½ dozen eggs home from the grocery store at 9:00 p.m., but couldn't find an egg in the house by breakfast time next morning: the boys had scrambled and eaten *all 30* for a bed-time snack! Our tender-hearted Benjamin celebrated his eighth birthday this month. Like a little border collie, Ben is constantly counting heads and corralling his younger siblings, making certain nobody gets lost or left behind. His big, puppy-dog eyes become deep pools of empathy whenever anyone gets hurt, and if it's Ben himself who's been injured, he tries as earnestly to calm and console those tending his wounds as they work to comfort and care for him.

November found Rachel potty-training and Isaac rolling over and saying "Mama." Jennifer stopped sewing window treatments for the new house long enough to make the requisite Pilgrim and Indian costumes we wore to our homeschool group's Thanksgiving Feast, complemented by moccasins, bows, and tomahawks the boys crafted themselves.... We decided to send this update a month early, to prevent its getting lost in the shuffle of the upcoming move, which appears to be just days away now. It has been exciting to see our new home materialize before our eyes, looking even better than we'd originally envisioned. As we turn our thoughts back to that stable in Bethlehem, though, we are reminded that *another* place is being prepared for us—and what a glorious mansion it must be, with over 2000 years in the making! As we celebrate the coming holiday season, we pray that each of you will put your faith and trust in the One whose sacrifice makes it possible for us to call heaven our eternal home: our Lord and Savior, Jesus Christ. For if *you confess with your mouth Jesus as Lord, and believe in your heart that God raised him from the dead, you shall be saved.* May God grant you a meaningful Christmas and a fruitful New Year. Let us hear from you soon!

With love from the Flanders family:
Doug, Jennifer, Jonathan, Bethany, David, Samuel, Benjamin,
Joseph, Rebekah, Rachel and Isaac

2004

It took several weeks for us to settle into our new home last December (if you want to update your directory, check the envelope for our new address). We moved every stick of furniture ourselves, including massive desks, heavy bookcases, and one unwieldy piano. The effort must've aged us considerably: some poor soul mistook Jennifer for Isaac's *grandmother* this month! The house is big (friends say we need walkie-talkies to carry on a conversation from opposite ends of the *master bedroom*); nevertheless, our little ones congregate in a dormer closet upstairs to play, Jon puts the top down on his Jeep and studies in the back seat, and the middle boys sleep in a pile on our den floor (cool weather) or in a tent in the woods behind our house (warm). We installed a water fountain on the back porch to keep the kids from running indoors every time they get thirsty, but the strategy backfired. Now when a child is *inside* and wants a drink, he jumps up and runs *outside* to get it!

Doug passed a 6mm kidney stone in January and was forced to call in sick for the first time *ever*, Bethany needed stitches after an antique water pitcher exploded in her hands, and Samuel had a pain in his side which required three doctors to rule out appendicitis. Good news is we met our insurance deductibles in record time this year! Bad news is we don't have dental: Isaac cut two teeth, Rebekah lost two, Jon got two pulled, Joe chipped one, Mom had a filling repaired, and David got braces. Even so, our oral discomfort did little to diminish any appetites. We had to scramble to keep that new 14-ft pantry well stocked. We'd buy ten gallons of milk and a dozen loaves of bread at a time, plus cereal, crackers, and canned goods by the case. And if Mom's confession that *"we're trying to heat our house with natural gas"* while purchasing 75 pounds of pinto beans weren't enough to raise a few eyebrows and humiliate a teenage son, her frantic search for a misplaced credit card—which she normally carries close to her heart—certainly did the trick!

David turned 12 in February. This sinewy left-hander with the size 14 foot has proven to be quite an athlete: he hit his first grand slam in baseball this spring, took first place in gold for his breaststroke this summer, and spends a good deal of his spare time lifting weights. The results are appreciable, particularly since he has only five percent body fat. Weary of seeing his brother flaunt those bulging biceps, Samuel once asked us to "tell David to quit moving his arms, because he's just doing it to show off his muscles!" While the charge was undoubtedly valid, we denied the request, just as we'd have done had someone suggested we "tell Sam to stop smiling, because he's just doing it to show off his dimples!" The boys had fun on the pogo stick Mom brought home from a yard sale this spring, but Samuel holds the record with 1100 consecutive bounces.

Doug's CME conferences took us to Addison for fondue and New Orleans for a swamp tour in March. It was great to come home to an empty "in box." Jennifer retired from Moms-Connect last month after seven years of sending daily e-news to over 400 home-schooling subscribers. Bethany served as an Azalea Belle again this year and had her picture in the paper several times in conjunction with that. She got her braces off just in time for the final photo shoot.

April took us to the Carolinas. When traffic came to a standstill on the outskirts of Savannah, we found ourselves trapped in the van with ten distended bladders and a father who

delights in cracking jokes at just such inopportune times. Doug's running commentary, delivered in a thick Irish brogue as he discreetly emptied bottles out the driver's side window, made our sides ache from laughter, but desperate times call for desperate measures. The girls waited for a service station, thank you very much, but regretted it after the attendant pointed them toward a dirty little broom closet with no lock, no toilet paper, no soap, and a handwritten sign on the wall which read, *"Aim for the toilet, not the floor."* Judging by how the ink had run, I'd say somebody aimed for the sign. We could feel the brush of angels' wings when we ran out of gas in the middle of a cloudburst, then managed to coast another half-mile down the highway, through a u-turn, across heavy traffic, and up an incline before rolling to a stop in front of the gas pump. We spent a relaxing afternoon kayaking at Hilton Head—at least it was relaxing for Mom, who held the baby, soaked up the scenery, and let the guide do all the work; the rest of the family had to paddle hard to keep up…. Jennifer packed the colonial costumes for us to wear in Old Salem (which we did), convinced we would blend right in (which we didn't). We could count on one hand the number of costumed interpreters we met during our off-season visit, and even *they* regarded us with puzzled expressions and asked loaded questions about our religious background, which they presumed must be very strict, indeed.

Isaac turned a year old in May. He took his first steps a few days before his birthday, but was so startled by all the whoops and whistles which attended this accomplishment that he made no further attempts to walk until mid-July! Instead, he worked overtime to hone those fine motor skills. He can now pry every last key off Jennifer's laptop in a matter of seconds (my "c" has never fully recovered) and has learned to separate double-ply tissue into single-ply while perched comfortably inside the toilet bowl, with knees to chest and seat up under his armpits…. Jonathan celebrated his 16th birthday this month. He participated in the volunteer program at Trinity Mother Frances this summer, served as a counselor at Diabetes Camp, taught water safety with the Red Cross, and swam competitively (as did Bethany, David, and Samuel) with the *Fun Forest Flying Fish*. With such a hectic schedule, it's no wonder Mom insisted on starting back to school a month early. She needed a break from summer break!

> — ❦ —
>
> *Bless us Lord,*
> *this Christmas,*
> *with quietness*
> *of mind;*
> *Teach us*
> *to be patient and*
> *always to be kind.*
>
> Helen Steiner Rice
>
> — ❦ —

The fact that our new house *echoes* lends validity to the children's oft-voiced complaint that it hurts their *ears* for Jennifer to sing and dance around the house, but Rachel added insult to injury by claiming it hurts her *eyes*, as well! This little sugarplum, who also answers to *"Boo"*, turned three in June. She loves to help Mommy in the kitchen, look at her scrapbook, and check the bounciness of her ponytails in our three-way mirror, although her enjoyment of this last activity has been severely curtailed since she lopped off the pigtails with a pair of Fiskars shortly after her birthday, just as both her sisters had done at the same age. Doug calls it their rite of passage. For Rachel, it has become an addiction, and her hair keeps getting steadily shorter, so if she's sporting a crew cut in next year's photo, you'll know why.

Family Camp at Crier Creek in July was a blast. Never one to do anything half-heartedly, Doug threw himself into the week's activities with abandon. The giant frog romper that Jennifer appliquéd for him to wear on "Flip-Flop" night drew lots of compliments from other campers, until they glimpsed the disposable diaper he was wearing underneath, its edges painted a convincing shade of mustard yellow, and lost their appetites. Jennifer took advantage of afternoon free-time to finish reading *Marriage to a Difficult Man*. Doug was concerned folks might assume this was a *how-to* book, but it's really a biography of Jonathan and Sarah Edwards, and one we'd highly recommend. Jon was old enough to accompany his dad on the cattle drive this year. With bandana, boots, and cowboy hat, Jonathan played the part better than Doug in his Maui Jims and Mizunos.

We started back to Cottage Garden in August, where Jennifer teaches a dozen students Logic and Charcoal Drawing (that's two different courses, in case you're grasping for a connection). David and Bethany both got blue ribbons at the East Texas State Fair for charcoal portraits they did as homework in Mom's class. Samuel took first place for a pillow he stitched for his bed and second place for a table he painted for the nursery. Benjamin, Joseph, Rebekah, and Rachel entered various drawings, paintings, pottery, embroidery, and papier-mâché, for which they earned a colorful array of ribbons, *including* several blue ones. Mom entered a piece of fillet crochet she framed for the dining room, but the year's biggest projects had to stay at home: frescos of fruit and vegetables painted on stone backsplashes in the kitchen, curtains for the bedroom windows, rooms faux-finished to look like they'd been wallpapered, a mosaic mirror and hand-painted sink for the guest bath, a painted rooster cabinet for the mudroom, and two pieces of stained glass for the master bathroom, which every child but Isaac helped solder together.

Our radiant Rebekah turned five in September. She enjoys reading, sewing, and testing the limits, which may explain her double-checking, "Am I allowed to eat *choking hazards?*" before answering our question of what she'd like to have for dinner. Joseph turned seven this

month. We knew we had been spending too much time in front of the big screen when our pastor described the parting of the Red Sea during a children's sermon, and Joe announced to everyone present, "*I saw that movie!*" He shares Dad's love for action/adventure flicks and Mom's love for art: passions which have produced such masterpieces as a full-length Spiderman costume he cut, colored, and stapled himself, and tenderly stores on a hanger in his closet when it's not being worn. Pen on paper is his preferred medium, but he'll use whatever materials are available. We've even seen him make gouache silhouettes using freshly chewed gum on a Pringles lid…. Bethany got her learner's permit the day she turned 15 and immediately took the wheel of our big white van. If learning to drive this mammoth vehicle were more nerve-wracking for her than for our firstborn, it was probably because she had to contend with a newly-licensed back-seat driver scrutinizing her every move (never mind the fact that Jonathan himself nearly *demolished a wall* trying to back out of the garage last January!).

Having finally saved enough frequent flyer miles to get ten free tickets to London, we spent the better part of October backpacking through Europe. Doug insisted we travel light, which in his mind meant *no socks* and only *two pair of underwear* (one to wash, one to wear). He wanted to leave room for more important things, like mime costumes to wear in Paris (I'm not kidding). This idea met with differing levels of enthusiasm. Samuel, who turned 11 this month, begged to dress as a mime for the entire trip, reasoning that if he only brought one outfit, he'd have no need for a backpack, and if he didn't talk, he could skip learning German, French, and Italian with the rest of the family. In the end, we packed a bit more than Doug thought necessary (which was fortuitous, as the extra layers kept us from freezing in the pre-dawn streets of Prague), but less than we'd have brought otherwise (which was a mercy, as Doug often carried the packs of his weary wife and/or young children in addition to his own). You shouldn't feel too sorry for him: Doug's was the only pack of 11 that came equipped with *wheels*, so it was seldom on his *back*. While the rest of us complained of burning shoulders and aching spines, he'd sympathize by telling us he had a cramp in his *thumb*! The trip was a great follow-up to our history studies: we saw the tower where Anne Boleyn lost her head, crowded into the attic where Anne Frank hid from the Nazis, stood on the spot where Charlemagne was crowned Holy Roman Emperor, admired the works of Michelangelo and Raphael (but missed Leonardo's), visited castles, cathedrals, concentration camps, and the Colosseum. Considering how many planes, trains, buses and boats we boarded/disembarked, it's a wonder we got separated only once, when the doors of a Frankfurt tram snapped shut with Mom, Dad, and two sleeping babies still inside, then sped away while our other seven children stood on a street corner and watched in dismay. Jon kept his siblings in line (literally) until we could make our way back to them, which we eventually did. Try as we might to wear dark colors and speak the language, there was no disguising the fact we were tourists, and a conspicuous lot, at that. We crowded into the kitchen of an Austrian guesthouse for breakfast and were greeted by another backpacker who smiled in recognition and told us, *"We saw your family at the Eiffel Tower last Tuesday!"* Jennifer spied a group of giggling boys hidden in the shadows of a dark alley in Salzburg and mistook them for her own sons. When they began howling like wolves, she played along by striking a Kung Fu pose and warning, "Stand back! I know karate!" At this point, the real Flanders showed up, and the wolves scampered downhill, praying the crazy lady did not give chase. Lucerne was a favorite stop, as much for the 10-bunk private dorm we occupied at the hostel as for the lovely vistas: quaint covered bridges spanning a lazy river, sidewalk cafés basking in the afternoon sun, and bright geraniums spilling out of window boxes at every turn. We clambered to the top of the clock tower in time to hear it strike noon, quite unexpectedly. The first deafening chime filled us with dread that the kids had *touched* something they shouldn't have. We were in Vienna for Austria's Independence Day: kids traveled free and shops were closed for the holiday, which was best for our budget on both counts. The Galleria in Milan was gorgeous, with its ornately carved shop-fronts and intricate mosaic floors. Having heard that the locals step on the testicles of Taurus for luck, we watched over breakfast to see if it were so. Sure enough, grown men would grind in their heels, little girls would dance and spin, college kids would pose for pictures, and even old women would carefully measure their steps, casting side-long glances to ensure a foot fell on that precise spot as they passed by. The canals *flooded* while we were in Venice. We sought refuge from the rain by attending Sunday mass (Basilicas are handier than Bible churches in Europe), but the water had risen so high by the end of the service that we had to *wade* back to the train station.

As remarkable as the things we *did* see in Europe, were the things we *didn't*: we never saw a squat-toilet (a fact for which we were so grateful, we didn't mind paying 80-cents a head to sit on the more familiar variety), we never encountered a rude Frenchmen (the Parisians we met were friendly and helpful, despite the fact we butchered their language every time we opened our mouths), and we were never bothered by pick-pockets (by journey's end, we looked like such an unwashed, unshaven band of vagabonds ourselves that thieves must've assumed we had no pockets worth picking, or feared we'd surround them, toss a baby in their arms, and rifle through *their* fanny-packs if they came too close!). Although we ate some delicious meals abroad, Benjamin (who turned nine on vacation) would tell you *his* favorite was one American Airlines served us during our flight home on November 3. In fact, we all enjoyed it, but it could've been the Captain's Announcing the Election Results that made it taste so sweet. As if to underscore the grace God had shown by keeping us healthy on our trip, Isaac got sick with a stomach virus the week after our return. It was short-lived—only took six days to make the rounds through our whole family— but by the time it had passed, we were over our jet lag and ready to hit the books with a fervor. This was nowhere more apparent than in Joseph, who begged to make up for lost time by doing five lessons a day. Jon got his hair cut (short!) and started working part-time at *Wild Birds Unlimited* and *Racquet&Jog*. Bethany became zealous about practicing the piano, so inspired was she by a classical concert we'd attended in the Czech Republic (although Isaac napped through this entire performance, he roused just long enough between pieces to *applaud* in his sleep). There was no gradual easing back into a routine for Doug: having been re-elected to a second term as president of his group, he shaved

> *From*
> *Home to home,*
> *and heart to heart,*
> *from one place*
> *to another.*
> *The warmth and joy*
> *of Christmas,*
> *brings us closer*
> *to each other.*
>
> Emily Matthews

off his month-old, salt-n-pepper beard and dove headfirst into anesthesia cases and contract negotiations. When he isn't at the hospital, you might spot him about town, looking like a cobbler in his wire-rimmed reading glasses, Swiss tunic, and Austrian vest. It's a good thing we didn't make it to Scotland—no telling what he'd be wearing!

Thanksgiving turkey polished off, blessings counted, and extended family members departed, we find ourselves facing December, eager to celebrate the blessed birth of our dear Savior and determined to get a jump-start on our New Year's resolutions. We pray that you will have a joyous and meaningful holiday season, as well, and that the risen Lord Jesus will reign in your hearts and homes in 2005. Let us hear from you soon!

With love from the Flanders family:
Doug, Jennifer, Jonathan, Bethany, David, Samuel, Benjamin,
Joseph, Rebekah, Rachel, and Isaac

Flanders Favorite Stocking Stuffers

If you were to visit us at Christmas time, you would find a long row of handmade felt stockings hanging from our mantle. We purposefully downplay the gifts around the tree. The kids exchange names to buy individual presents, and I usually wrap a family gift that we can all enjoy, like a new game or a book to read at story time. But the main event at our house Christmas morning is emptying our stockings. We take turns, youngest to oldest, as the rest of the family watches. Stocking stuffers vary a lot with age and sex, but here's a list of some of our kids' favorites from Christmases past:

- baby rattles
- pacifiers
- bouncy balls
- brightly colored links
- Beenie Babies or other small stuffed animals
- Matchbox cars
- Crayola crayons
- coloring books
- Barbie dolls
- flashcards (for school)
- card games
- mini Lego figures
- new combs
- blow-dart guns (with rubber-tipped darts)
- hair scrunchies, bows, ribbons, and barrettes
- travel soaps, lotions, and shampoo

- Band-Aids
- deodorant
- hairbrushes
- nail clippers
- nail polish
- lip gloss
- homemade coupons for special outings or privileges
- washable markers
- Scotch tape
- Disney stickers
- candy canes
- gummy bears
- harmonicas
- new socks
- new underwear
- whole mixed nuts (still in the shell)
- personalized return address labels

- Smoothie King gift cards
- pocket calculator
- miniature flashlights
- beef jerky
- apples and oranges (great for filling the toe)
- new razors
- new toothbrushes
- breath mints
- Starbuck's coupons
- personalized stationery or thank-you notes
- postage stamps
- new pens or pencils
- small sewing kit
- mini-staplers
- colored pencils
- granola bars
- trail mix
- small Sudoku books

2005

      We hosted Doug's office party last December, giving Jennifer a good excuse to furnish the upstairs, which had stood nearly empty for almost a year. The event was a great success, due primarily to the wonderful food catered by the head chef of Mercy Ships—everything was so delicious, no one seemed to mind the fact we didn't serve alcohol. We learned the following week that Jennifer was expecting again, which was the best Christmas gift we could imagine. Second best were the Harvest of Hope gift certificates we received from Jennifer's sister's family. These, combined with money that the kids contributed from their own savings, allowed us to buy a goat for a family in China, dig a well for a village in Africa, provide school supplies and medical care for children in the Middle East, and build a house for a family in Indonesia. We know of few ministries that can do so much with so little.

      The weather was mild enough in January to do some of our lessons outdoors: the boys spread quilts in the backyard, pulled off their T-shirts, and basked in the sun while Mom read G.A. Henty aloud, at least until the sprinklers came on unexpectedly and sent us scurrying for cover. Isaac learned to sleep through the night this month, Rachel learned to pump herself on a swing, and Rebekah (thanks to David) learned to ride a bike without training wheels. Jonathan and Bethany practiced all month before taking the SAT—their last opportunity to do so before an essay section was added. We unwound after the test by spending a few days in San Antonio, where Jennifer and the kids took in all the sights while Doug attended an army conference.

      Bethany drove the girls to Mesquite for our annual mother/daughter Valentine's brunch. Dad stayed at home and took advantage of our absence to smuggle a few items to Goodwill, including Jennifer's favorite bicycle. The boys warned him not to do it, thinking she would be upset, but Mom showed genuine delight over the replacement she found waiting in the rack when she got back home (if she's learned anything in 18 years of marriage, it's that resistance is futile, anyway). David turned 13 this month. He came to breakfast one morning looking an inch taller than the day before, a fact his mother noticed immediately, since he was no longer at eye level. "It's funny you should mention it," he told her, "because when I was trying to go to sleep last night, it felt like my skin was too tight for my bones." We used a tape measure to verify, and sure enough, he'd passed both Mom and Jon and was rapidly closing in on Beth (he would overtake her and catch up to Dad by year's end).

Doug began giving away most of his weekend call in March, which left more time to enjoy such springtime activities as tennis and board game tournaments, family bike rides, and two separate campouts with homeschooling friends (not nearly the hassle now that our big, strapping boys can pack supplies, drive down early, pitch tents, inflate air-mattresses, and cook dinner, so the only thing left for us latecomers to do is to fall into bed and let the crickets lull us to sleep). Doug spent two weekends in Houston doing CME this month, but was back in town to stitch up the gaping, three-inch gash Benjamin took to his shin trying to hurdle a brick wall, and was also around to help get the van to a service station when Jennifer ran out of gas at a busy intersection. Unbeknownst to us, one of Doug's co-workers witnessed *that* spectacle from his car and took pictures with a cell phone to circulate at the hospital for

laughs. These didn't get the reaction he expected. When folks saw the snapshots of Doug, his pregnant wife, and a bevy of youngsters straining to push our van across Broadway, they chastised the photographer for not lending a hand! Still, everyone had to admit, we *did* look funny.

The time change wreaked havoc with the children's schedules in April. Isaac woke up at two o'clock every morning bright-eyed and bushy-tailed, then Benjamin would try (unsuccessfully) to drag Mom out of bed at four to do school. Even with her putting him off until 5:30, he'd finish most of his work in time to join big brothers on the tennis courts at dawn. The middle boys played baseball this spring. Joseph hit a home run in the final inning one week, bringing in two extra runners to win the game. While the other players patted him on the back, he gathered a bouquet of wildflowers for Mom. Presenting it to her afterwards, he asked, "Do you know what I love even more than baseball? *My family.*" Doug turned 38 this month and celebrated having now known Jennifer half his life. Jennifer expected to be tormented about turning 40, but she didn't hear a single snide remark (then again, warns her sister, your *hearing* is usually the first thing to go). Instead, she received lots of hugs and kisses, plus a family night at the movies. We arrived early for the grand opening of the new Carmike Theater ($2 tickets, including snacks). Our little ones sat still for almost an hour, munching complimentary popcorn and waiting for the feature to begin, but by the time it actually started, the unlimited free sodas had run their course, so Mom had to supervise a seemingly endless string of potty breaks. When she finally returned to her seat, Isaac set to squirming with such vigor that she gave up seeing the show altogether and took the baby shopping until it was over. Doug and the older kids expressed regret over how the evening turned out, but Jennifer assured them she'd choose motherhood over uninterrupted movies, any day of the week…. We were still struggling to make good our New Year's resolution to be on time for church when we began opening our home this month to a few like-minded families for Sunday worship and fellowship dinner. Word spread, and our congregation grew. By June, we were averaging 100 in weekly attendance, so we bought a bunch of folding chairs, got licensed to project song lyrics overhead, hooked a microphone up to our speaker system, and hauled in a cattle trough for conducting baptisms in the driveway. It has been an incredible blessing to watch God work and to observe His perfect timing and provision in all things. And as an added bonus, our family has never been late to services since (a record we hope to maintain once the church moves into a bigger building the Sunday after Thanksgiving).

> — ❧✳❧ —
>
> *A Christmas candle is a lovely thing; It makes no noise at all, But softly gives itself away; While quite unselfish, it grows small.*
>
> Eva K. Logue
>
> — ❧✳❧ —

We celebrated Cinco de Mayo (05/05/05) with a trip to Six Flags for Homeschool Day. The park was full of friendly faces, and we bumped into folks we knew at every turn. Isaac turned two in May. He loves to arm wrestle and eagerly flops belly-down on the ground, elbow planted firmly in front of him, to challenge any and all passers-by. He is thus far undefeated, as none of us can resist the sound of his laughter when he wins. Isaac is also fond of digging in the garden, wearing wristwatches, and starting knock-knock jokes (though he's yet to learn any punch lines)…. Jennifer was so impressed with Debi Pearl's new book, *Created To Be His Help Meet*, she ordered two dozen copies to give to friends. We've since passed out an additional eight *cases* and plan to make it required reading for all our daughters and future daughters-in-law before they'll be allowed to marry…. Doug arranged for an armada of new cars to be delivered mid-month and the not-so-old ones hauled away. The new vehicles are actually leases, which I suppose makes sense for anyone who trades them in as often as Doug. It certainly keeps Jennifer guessing—no telling how much time she has spent in crowded parking lots, hunting a van we no longer own. Jonathan turned 17 this month. He worked at *Racquet&Jog* all summer, but left in September after a dentist at church offered him a job in his new Tyler office. Dentistry has replaced trauma surgery as Jonathan's career of choice, and he was chomping at the bits to begin training. Mom and Dad came home from a date one evening to find Jon decked out in a surgical mask and latex gloves, a tray full of pliers at his side, one brother laid before him in an easy chair and the others lined up on the couch watching and waiting their turn. He had taken it upon himself to extract every loose tooth in the house, and—what's more incredible—the owners of those teeth were cooperating!

Rachel celebrated her fourth birthday in June. She enjoys singing, helping in the kitchen, and taking gymnastics. She also loves to draw and would do so in her sleep if Mom would allow, which she no longer does, since it makes such a mess when the pen wanders off the paper onto her pillowcase during the night…. Isaac nearly choked to death on a donut hole this month. He wouldn't be with us today were it not for God's mercy, Bethany's vigilance, and Mom's quick reflexes. Jennifer was still shaking hours after the incident, but Isaac was begging for more to eat almost as soon as the obstruction was cleared…. Our oldest two children spent a week at World View Academy in Waco, their first time away from the rest of the family. The little ones cried when they learned their siblings were leaving, but had apparently adjusted by dinnertime. We were enjoying a quiet meal at a local cafeteria when Jennifer overheard Joe announce, "I claim Jonathan's bike!" and Rebekah add, "I get Bethany's!" Appalled that they could turn so easily from *missing* their brother and sister to *calling dibs* on their possessions, Mom interrupted the conversation to ask what in the world they would do with such big bikes if they *had* them. Puzzled, they answered in unison, "We'd *eat* them." Turns out Mom had misunderstood: instead of *bikes*, they were discussing *bites*, as in forkfuls of Dad's dessert, which he always splits with the kids. Joseph and Rebekah just wanted to make sure the nibbles normally reserved for Jon and Beth did not go to waste in their absence!

July brought the cutest family of armadillos to our backyard every morning at nine o'clock, which the children took great delight in watching forage through our flowerbeds. We could squat within a foot of them without their seeming to notice. July also brought new neighbors—a family with three small boys and three big dogs moved in next door, and since the day they arrived, Isaac has considered their house his home away from home…. Doug had worked eight months with no vacation by the time Family Camp rolled around, so we were *all* glad to get away to Crier Creek for a week of R&R. The girls at camp asked Jennifer to give an afternoon talk on the topic of organization this year, and she jumped at the opportunity. She saved all her notes, and if she ever finds time to organize *those*, she may publish. We stayed in Houston for a few days after camp to put Bethany on a plane for England. Her SAT scores landed her an invitation to study at Cambridge this summer, and she flew into London just a week after the subways were bombed. Figuring out what to do when neither the credit card PIN nor her long-distance calling card would work overseas was almost as challenging as her coursework in political theory, British history, and debate. She stayed busy studying for class, making friends, going on field trips, and taking lessons in punting, fencing, and salsa dancing, but still found time to feel homesick.

It seems our new baby was not in as big a hurry to meet us as we were to meet him. We waited patiently for an extra week before inducing labor on August 16. Daniel Prescott Flanders was born 3½ hours later, at 11:02 a.m.—a whopping 9 lbs 13 oz and 21 inches long. Daddy caught the baby, and Samuel cut the cord. He has Papa Cowan's big hands, but otherwise looks just like his brothers. Prescott was Jennifer's idea—it's an Old English name that means "from the priest's cottage," making it a fitting marker for the year the church spent meeting in our home. Daniel is as sweet as sugar. Before he was a week old, Jennifer overheard Doug boasting that the baby had already learned to sleep through the night. In reality, it was Doug who'd reached *that* milestone—baby was still waking up three or four times a night to nurse, but kept quiet enough even when hungry that Dad's rest was seldom disturbed.

Forewarned that his group's contract with Mother Frances would not be renewing next July, Doug put our house on the market in September.

> *The merry*
> *family gatherings—*
> *The old, the very young;*
> *The strangely lovely*
> *way they*
> *Harmonize in carols sung.*
> *For Christmas is*
> *tradition time—*
> *Traditions that recall*
> *The precious memories*
> *down the years,*
> *The sameness of them all.*
>
> Helen Lowrie Marshall

Despite the rumor that our family is moving to Australia (a remote possibility publicized by our more adventurous children), we are actually just trying to live a yielded life: if the house sells, we'll faithfully follow God's lead elsewhere; if it doesn't, we'll joyfully serve Him here. Nevertheless, the decision meant signing contracts with realtors, fielding questions from neighbors and friends, and keeping the house ready to show at a moment's notice—tasks Doug left to his postpartum wife while he conveniently disappeared for two weeks of Army Reserve duty in El Paso (and, yes, she's forgiven him his poor timing)! Jennifer was sick in bed with mastitis the day Rebekah turned six, so her siblings took over the party plans. Her brothers bought gifts (Ninja Turtles and bouncy balls), Bethany baked a strawberry cake, and Benjamin converted our driveway into a wading pool. This attracted the neighbor boys, who were happy to help us celebrate and share birthday cake. Bethany turned 16 this month, and a sweeter sixteen we've never known. She didn't complain about Dad's being out of town for the big day, or about her biology professor's scheduling a major exam that morning, or about Mom's packing the family into a hotel so our floors could be refinished, and when a friend invited her over to celebrate, she declined, explaining that she didn't want to burden her mother with such a request during what was already so stressful a time. The irony is that her self-sacrificing efforts to relieve Jennifer's stress actually compounded it, for the invitation was in reality a ploy to keep Beth occupied so Mom and the kids could decorate for her surprise party, which was ultimately a success even *without* her cooperation. Our inquisitive Joseph turned eight this month. He has requested that we make India our next vacation destination, so he can observe *tigers* in their natural habitat. Can't you just see it now, the Flanders in matching khakis and pith helmets, exploring the jungles of South Asia? But alas, our years of flexible, off-season travel may have come to an end, as Jonathan and Bethany began dual-credit courses at Tyler Junior College this fall. Now we'll have to schedule our vacations around a school calendar, like the rest of the world.

Bethany did manage to squeeze a ten-day trip to Qatar into her schedule this October, serving as a nanny for friends who are considering a move to the Middle East. She returned home heavy-laden with souvenirs for the family, including a couple of dolls wrapped head-to-toe in black burkas for Rachel and Rebekah, who barely recognized Barbie in such modest attire! Benjamin and Samuel celebrated their tenth and twelfth birthdays this month, respectively. They spend most of their free time skateboarding, playing chess, perfecting their tennis and ping-pong games, and practicing the piano—or, in Sam's case, the violin. We made two trips to the emergency room this month: first, when Doug developed another kidney stone which had to be surgically removed; second, when Isaac fell down the stairs and broke his collar bone. Forty-eight hours after Doug's procedure, he pulled the stint, questioning whether his body would *ever* fully recover (it did ☺). Forty-eight hours after Isaac's accident, we found him swinging by both arms from the clothes rod in his closet, ready to move on to his *next* injury.

November took us to San Antonio for Doug's 20-year high school reunion. We so enjoyed reconnecting with old friends that we're planning to meet them again next summer in San Diego. We spent a lazy afternoon in Gruene, Texas. Papa joined Doug and the boys on the Guadalupe, towing their tubes behind his canoe over the slower parts of the river. Nana and Bethany took the girls window-shopping in shifts, while Jennifer enjoyed some peace and quiet at a nearby park, working on a cross-stitched sampler as she watched the babies sleep and the little ones climb trees. We learned upon our return home that the father of a dear friend had passed away. He was a godly man, committed to making his life count for Christ. His memorial service challenged us to do likewise, for our days are also fleeting.

December seems to come earlier every year. Our Christmas cruise to Belize was cancelled in the wake of Hurricanes Katrina and Rita, a much less devastating loss than many suffered, especially considering Carnival refunded our money in full. We'll spend the holidays closer to home, thankful that our extended families can still be together. The younger children will be participating in a nativity play at a local nursing home this month. The boys are shepherds, the girls are angels, and Daniel is the baby in the manger. As we again celebrate the birth of our blessed Savior, it is our prayer that others will find Jesus not only in the stable and at the cross, but also on the throne of our hearts. May He bless you and yours with a joyous Christmas and a fruitful New Year! We look forward to hearing from you soon.

With love from the Flanders family:
Doug and Jennifer, Jonathan, Bethany, David, Samuel, Benjamin, Joseph, Rebekah, Rachel, Isaac, and Daniel

- Our Christmas Card Assembly Line -

Our family sends out over 200 Christmas cards each year, and getting them ready to mail is a joint effort. We set up shop at a long table and churn them out in fast order. Every member of the family is given a task. As our family has grown, we've had to manufacture extra "jobs" for the assembly line. Now we have several kids in charge of stamps and stickers. One will put large stickers on the back of the envelope, another will put small stickers on the front. One will rubber stamp with red ink, another will use a different stamp with green, and yet another will use a tiny, self-inking stamp that says "Merry Christmas."

We usually listen to Christmas music while we work and have hot cocoa once we're done. Even our college kids still love to help and ask us to assemble on a night they can participate, usually over Thanksgiving break.

A couple years ago, I smiled to hear one of these older kids say, "It's a good thing we have so many helpers in this family. Can you imagine how long it would take one person to do all this alone?" He was too young to know that there was once a time (over 20 years ago) when Mom did do the job alone, addressing all the envelopes by hand and sending them unembellished. The task is much more fun now that we do it together! Here's how our job assignments are currently broken down:

- ➢ Put address labels on envelopes.
- ➢ Affix postage stamps to envelopes.
- ➢ Emboss envelope flap.
- ➢ Put small stickers on front of envelope.
- ➢ Put large sticker on back of envelope.
- ➢ Rubber stamp envelope with red ink.
- ➢ Rubber stamp envelope with green ink.

- ➢ Put labels on backs of photos.
- ➢ Fold Christmas letters.
- ➢ Stuff envelope.
- ➢ Add handwritten notes as desired.
- ➢ Double check that all is in order.
- ➢ Seal envelope.
- ➢ Place finished letter in mail bucket.

2006

It's a good thing we mailed the Christmas letters *early* last year—our assembly-line would have been short-handed had we waited any longer, since Jon was hospitalized after Thanksgiving for the first time in 16 years. A severe staph infection took three weeks of IV antibiotics and lots of prayer to overcome, but he was discharged in time for finals at TJC and passed with flying colors despite his absences—another answer to prayer. Both our extended families gathered in Grapevine for a few days of sightseeing and fine dining before following us home for Christmas. Isaac loved the gift he got from his big brothers—a one-piece, spandex Spiderman suit which fastens up the back. He wore it constantly, layered beneath pajamas and play-clothes alike. Such preparedness may save time for superheroes, but it tends to make diaper changes unnecessarily difficult.

Resolving to spend more time with the family and less at the office, Doug tendered his resignation as president of East Texas Anesthesia Associates in January. The vice-president agreed to take over early, but claimed that "succeeding Flanders feels like following Babe Ruth at bat." As per our custom, the kids swapped chore assignments for the New Year. Samuel got laundry duty, giving him a better appreciation for that never-ending task. He'd been washing three loads a day for a week when Mom caught him playing football with his brothers in the backyard one crisp winter morning wearing nothing but a T-shirt, underwear, and a skateboard helmet. When she questioned the scant dress, Samuel explained, "I didn't want to *waste* my clean clothes!"

Our 6'4" bottomless pit turned 14 on February 20. No longer content to polish off a full box of cereal or carton of eggs as a midnight snack, now when David gets hungry after dinner, he'll bake ten loaves of bread and *eat two* while they're still warm. You wouldn't know it to look at him. He stays fit riding his bicycle, pedaling over 80 miles at a stretch. Our entire family logged some good mileage on foot this month in preparation for the Cowtown Half-Marathon. Doug, Jennifer, Jon, Bethany, David, and Samuel stretched their long run to ten miles, while the little ones joined us for shorter runs, riding on bikes or in strollers. We made it to Fort Worth just ahead of a thunderstorm. It raged all night and was still pouring at race time next morning, so we decided to forfeit. The boys were terribly disappointed, and the girls were secretly relieved (but don't tell).

We joined an organic vegetable co-op in March which specializes in crops we never knew existed: white radishes, purple kale, black bell peppers, yellow chard, and a variety of greens we still can't identify but have grown to like. Of necessity, Mom's cooking skills have been stretched to the point that our family eats almost all our meals at home anymore, usually without complaints. Doug's willingness to forgo restaurant dinners may be due in part to his preoccupation with a little construction project he and the boys tackled on his days off. They designed a massive tree fort with three stories, which Doug jokingly dubbed the "family practice level, the orthopedic level, and the neurosurgical level" (referring to the kind of specialist we'd need should anyone fall from a given deck). In the end, better judgment prevailed and they stopped with two, the second of which is kept secured with a combination lock when not in use. Still, it's a nice place to read a book or gaze at the stars, and it makes a terrific launch pad for the zip line Uncle Chris installed last December.

That project complete, Doug was even less interested in moving than he'd been before. Our house showed a few times in April, but we took it off the market when it hadn't sold by summer, which explains why we're still here, and happily so. We *did* sell our Rolexes, but they weren't the hassle to pack nor was our emotional attachment as strong. Doug re-instituted story time now that he is home most evenings. He read *Swallows and Amazons* aloud to the children, then sent them to bed and swapped interesting excerpts from other books with Jennifer while soaking in the tub. Favorite picks this year include Mark Kurlansky's *Salt*, Jared Diamond's *Collapse*, Ann Coulter's *Godless*, John Piper's *Don't Waste Your Life*, and Milo Frank's *How to Get Your Point Across in 30 Seconds or Less* (which we've successfully applied to everything but Christmas letters).

Our indefatigable Isaac turned three on May 22 and inherited the Davy Crockett costume Mom had made for *Jon's* third birthday. It has been passed from brother to brother for the past 15 years, but the latest recipient wore it only two days before reverting back to his Spidey suit. Isaac loves to help around the house, so Dad showed him how to use an electric paper shredder to dispose of junk mail. In retrospect, this was a bad idea. The stack of "pre-approved credit" offers ran out long before Isaac's enthusiasm for the task, so he cracked open the permanent files and began shredding Doug's tax receipts! Our two oldest kids graduated from high school this month and received their diplomas during our homeschool group's annual commencement exercises. It was early for Bethany, but she'd been doing the same coursework as Jon since ninth grade, so it made sense (at least until Mom realized she'd be leaving for college in a few months and began to second-guess the decision). Bethany independently arrived at the same conclusion—that 16 is too young to move away from home—so she postponed applying to Dallas Baptist University in favor of spending her first two years at Tyler Junior College, where she was awarded a full presidential scholarship and a job as a biology lab assistant. Jonathan decided to stay at TJC, as well, not because he has any qualms about leaving home—he's been planning an exit strategy for months now—but because he can't bear the thought of living more than ten minutes away from his fellow Red Cross volunteer and sweetheart of two years, the lovely and loveable Matti Jones. He grew a goatee after celebrating his 18th birthday on May 31. It has served as a good visual reminder for us to treat him like an adult. Learning to *let go* has been particularly challenging for Mom (who distinctly remembers crying when Jonathan was four days old, because he was growing up so *fast*), so Doug made her practice repeating, *"Okay, Sweetie. Have fun. I love you. See you when you get home..."* until she could say it in her sleep. That has actually helped. Do you suppose this will get any easier as our last ones leave the nest?

> *The joy of brightening other lives, bearing each others' burdens, easing other's loads and supplanting empty hearts and lives with generous gifts becomes for us the magic of Christmas.*
>
> W. C. Jones

Our radiant Rachel turned five on June 16. This little monkey enjoys climbing, singing, and (especially) drawing. She can occupy herself for hours given a copious supply of paper and a ballpoint pen. She loves her mommy, but she *adores* her big sister—so much so that she once asked her siblings, "Don't you wish *Beth* could be our mother?" When the others urged her to recant, Rachel remained adamant: "But Bethany's so *nice*—she gives us candy, her face is prettier, and she draws better!" Jennifer took it in stride. If *she'd* had a big sister like Bethany at that age, *she* might have felt the same way.... The Army Reserve called Doug up for another four months, this time to El Paso, so our whole family piled in the van and headed west for the summer. It was a trick to fit all twelve of us into the 500 ft^2 apartment he was assigned (an area roughly the size of our back porch), but it was carpeted, so Daniel finally learned how to crawl cross-pattern, instead of the belly-swim he'd been doing across our hardwood floors back home. The kitchen, which we shared with another soldier, had just enough room for a card table and single chair, so we ate our meals at a picnic table across the parking lot. Our only three-pronged outlet was in the tiny bathroom that consequently doubled as our home office. We had to squeeze between sink and shower *sideways* to reach it, but once there, we could sit on the toilet, spit in the sink, and check our e-mail, all at the same time. An aquatic center two blocks away afforded a roomier way to bathe the kids and was a welcome respite from the heat. All the children from Rebekah up joined the swim team and practiced daily. Doug had weekends off, which provided a great opportunity to explore the American Southwest. We spent spare moments museum hopping, rock climbing, mountain biking, whitewater rafting, sand dune sliding, spelunking, and sampling lots of spicy Mexican food. The children's requests to dine at familiar chain restaurants fell on deaf ears as Doug insisted we scout out every mom-and-pop establishment west of the Rio Grande in an effort to "soak up local culture" (he was not opposed to sharing a little culture of our own, however, which explains his volunteering Jennifer to sing Mozart's *Queen of the Night* aria with an amused but accommodating mariachi/karaoke band). Jon, Beth, and David spent three weeks at language school in Costa Rica this month, so they enjoyed the added adventure of going on canopy tours, sea turtle rescues, and lobster dives. Eager to have them home, we arrived at the airport a day early to meet their plane and were crestfallen to discover they weren't on it (nor were they supposed to be). Rebekah even cried.

David, Samuel, and Doug competed in their first triathlon in July, placing third, fourth, and fifth in their respective age divisions (which sounds more impressive than citing the fact that only a single runner crossed the finish line *behind* them). Since the race was a sprint, the distances were short, and their muscles weren't sore the following day. Heady from the sense of accomplishment, they were soon searching the Internet for Ironman dates and tips on improving their time. Doug began what he called his *Kenyan Diet* after reading a breakdown of what the fastest runners in the world eat during training. Never mind that these athletes are 20 years younger, six inches shorter, and 100 pounds lighter—it's the *cornmeal and sweet tea* that gives them their edge!

Even as the drought at home was turning our lawn a crispy brown, El Paso was getting more rain than it had seen since the 1800's. Parts of downtown had to be evacuated in August

> *Perhaps the best Yuletide decoration is being wreathed in smiles.*
>
> Anonymous

when the Rio Grande overran its banks and a dam across the border threatened to unleash another six million gallons of water on the already distressed city. Our family was confined to Fort Bliss until after the storms subsided, but Doug came up with a capital way to combat cabin fever. He'd drive us around the base until he spotted a tempting puddle, then slip on his sunglasses (despite heavy cloud cover), rev the engine (pretending to challenge any oncoming traffic or hapless pedestrians), and peel across deserted streets and empty parking lots, leaving a wall of water in his wake. The wife and kids would roar with laughter and beg him to do it again and again. Once the sun came back out, we worked double-time to fit in all the sightseeing we still wanted to do before Jennifer and the children headed for home. We toured pecan farms, grape orchards, turquoise shops, salt flats, Mexican markets, National Parks, a glass factory, a candy plant, and several zoos. Benjamin helped conduct electricity for a Tesla coil demonstration, Mom and Dad wrestled a 120-pound boa constrictor during a reptile show, and the twelve-and-under crowd earned a bunch of badges in the Junior Ranger program. We were received warmly everywhere we went, with the exception of one museum in Las Cruces, where the little old ladies who served as volunteer docents seemed completely unnerved by our big brood. *"Get away from that exit! You'll set off the alarm! Don't pet the cows! Two at a time on the seesaw! For Heaven's sake, stay away from that display—it's an antique!"* We were called down for various offenses no less than six times before Jennifer, red with humiliation, packed up the kids and drove back to El Paso in tears. She *hates* getting in trouble.

Doug's tour of duty lasted another five weeks after the family moved home to start school, so he missed our wedding anniversary and several birthdays, to boot. Daniel turned one on August 16: A curly-headed boy with a winning smile, he has eight teeth now, three of which he cut in El Paso while battling a horrendous case of thrush. Breastfeeding would've surely gone by the wayside had there been any other way to keep baby quiet behind those paper-thin walls of the bachelor barracks. Jennifer spent several nights sleeping in the van with him, as it was. Rebekah turned seven on September 9: In addition to a strong will and sharp mind, she has her mother's gift for music. She began piano lessons this fall, rehearses faithfully, and thinks *having-to-practice* is as urgent a reason to postpone bedtime as *needing-to-potty*. Jennifer's parents drove out to surprise us on Rebekah's birthday, bringing a book of Sudoku puzzles with them. We had fun racing to see who could finish first (Samuel and Bethany won by wide margins). Joseph turned nine September 11: He is creative, resourceful, and brave about trying new things. Now that Jon's moved upstairs to the guest room (fewer distractions when he's trying to study), Joseph and David have a room to themselves, unless you count Crystal, Joe's little stuffed dog and constant companion. Joseph's skill with a needle and thread has turned that pup into quite the clotheshorse. Beth turned 17 on September 20: She's a bit of a clothes horse herself, although much of her wardrobe no longer fits. Her long hours at the gym have finally paid off, so instead of *gaining fifteen* pounds her freshman year, she *dropped forty*.... The *Tyler Morning Telegraph* ran an article on homeschooling this fall and sent reporters to our house to get pictures for the story. Doug spent two hours fielding questions about why we do what we do. Short answer: No, we're not reacting to some bad experience in our childhoods. We loved school, loved our teachers, and are grateful for the education we received in the public school system. But we also love our children, love learning, and enjoy doing it together. Homeschooling is not the *only* way to fulfill the Biblical injunction to teach "when you sit in your house, when you walk by the way, when you lie down, and when you rise up" (Deuteronomy 6:4-9), but it's certainly a *rewarding* way to do so, and fosters family friendships, besides.... David took the training wheels off Rachel's bicycle this month and taught her to ride without them. He has become

the little ones' go-to guy for bike help, as well as first aid. Doug, Sam, and Ben have begun joining David on treks with the Tyler Biking Club. The four ride to Bullard almost every Saturday morning to eat breakfast at Sherry's Kitchen. But life is not always so idyllic. Three short months after being diagnosed with stomach cancer, Jennifer's father passed away on September 20. It was a shock. None of us were ready to lose him, but by grace through faith, he was ready to go. They say that children tend to view God in the same way they view their dad. Perhaps that is true. My earthly father was wise, benevolent, and completely trustworthy, so it has never been difficult for me to trust implicitly in the wisdom, goodness, and faithfulness of my Heavenly Father. And *that's* a rich heritage, indeed.

But *time stands still for no man.* The day after we buried Papa, Jonathan paid off the wedding set he had chosen for Matti and, with the blessing of both sets of parents, proposed in October. Yes, they're young; yes, they'll face hardships; but life is short; and postponing marriage often presents challenges of its own. Jonathan and Matti both love the Lord and are committed to building their home on His Word, so we are excited for them. They opted to make it a short engagement—just six weeks—which means they'll be on their honeymoon by the time you receive this letter! Our sober-minded Samuel turned 13 on October 2 and joined the ballroom dance class, something he's wanted to do since his older siblings started lessons a year ago. In true Renaissance fashion, he plays the violin and tennis and throws himself into his studies, as well. Sam loves the sciences and would rather read *ten* biology texts than a single work of fiction. He also loves the baby. At his request, we attached a child-carrier to his bike, so he can pump Daniel around the neighborhood in the afternoons and keep him from getting underfoot while Mom cooks dinner. Incidentally, the baby took his first step this month and is now walking *everywhere*. It is so sweet to watch him toddle around the house with his arms outstretched and a smile across his face. He is understandably proud of the accomplishment, as are we all…. Benjamin turned 11 on October 16. A hard worker, he considers any amount of physical labor a good excuse to strip off his shirt and flaunt his "six-pack." Ben is gregarious and loves to be on the go, but has become much more focused in his lessons this year after learning that Joseph might catch him in a couple of subjects—there's nothing like a little sibling rivalry to light the fire under a procrastinator (at least, that's how it worked when Jennifer was in school—she'd never have graduated summa cum laude from DBU had she not glimpsed those straight A's her sister Kimberly kept bringing home)!

> ——— ❧✳☙ ———
>
> *Happy, happy Christmas, that can win us back to the delusions of our childhood days, recall to the old man the pleasures of his youth, and transport the traveler back to his own fireside and quiet home!*
>
> Charles Dickens
>
> ——— ❧✳☙ ———

The weather turned decidedly cooler in November, making us grateful for the ample supply of firewood Doug and the boys laid up this fall. They cleared all the dead trees off our property using Dad's new chain saw and Papa's old axe, and then raced to see who could split the logs the fastest. Neither Jon nor Samuel could bear being bested by a 14-year old brother, and their repeated attempts to out-do David got the job finished in short order…. Unwilling to wait for January, Doug made "Reformation Day Resolutions" this year. In addition to writing, exercising, taking vitamins, and *religiously* tracking calories, he has sworn off caffeine (again), refined sugar (except gum), and fried foods (not including maple-flavor bacon). He is busily training for another triathlon, having set as his goal being ready for the Half-Ironman in Dallas on his 40th birthday. Several of our kids plan to compete in various events that same weekend, but Jennifer is hoping to be pregnant by then, which will give her a good excuse to sit this one out.

That wraps up our news for another year—it blew by so fast that our heads are spinning. As December turns our thoughts back to the birth of our Savior, we pray Jesus will reign in your heart and home this Christmas and grant you peace and prosperity in 2007. Let us hear from you soon!

With love from the Flanders family:
Doug and Jennifer, Jon (and Matti), Bethany, David, Samuel,
Benjamin, Joseph, Rebekah, Rachel, Isaac, and Daniel

Photo by Molly Bodenhamer

And they all lived happily ever after . . .

2007

"What's with all the hatchets and machetes?" That's what Jon wanted to know when he and Matti dropped by last December to find the entire family working in the woods behind our house. We'd been spending Saturday mornings raking leaves, clearing underbrush, felling trees, and hauling firewood. Even Baby Daniel got in on the action by carrying small logs and kindling to the back porch. The newlyweds arrived just in time to watch Doug make assignments and distribute tools. Jon was incredulous. Pointing to a little sister hacking earnestly at a vine, he reminded his father, "You wouldn't even let me carry a *pocket knife* when *I* was that age!" I guess he's right—times *have* changed. (Just wait until he sees all the Airsoft rifles his brothers bought this fall).

Progress was slow and the weather turned cold, so in January we hired professionals to finish the job. Note to self: Next time warn the neighbors—the cardiologist's wife next door nearly had a heart attack when she spotted all those strangers prowling around behind her property. Some homemade muffins and spicy taquitos helped smooth the misunderstanding, and the men returned to work with fervor. Within three days, they'd raked every leaf, hauled off all the brush piles, and ground countless stumps. David, Sam and Ben spent another three days meticulously spreading 200 bales of pine needles over the entire acre and a half. Whenever Mom or Dad grabbed a rake and tried to help, the boys shooed us away, preferring the more even results they achieved by sifting the straw through their fingers. The land looked pristine once they finished.

We found out in February that our first grandbaby was on the way! Matti got pregnant about a week after Jon's insurance kicked in—how's *that* for impeccable timing? She looked radiant, despite her terrible morning sickness…. David turned 15. He's 6'5" now and solid muscle. He loves to swim, bike, run, read, and practice the piano—and believes the *faster* he can do those things, the better. He plays Mozart's *Turkish March* a hundred times a day at such heart-pounding tempos that his fingers are a blur…. Doug took the older kids to Longview this month for the aptly-named *Freeze Your Fanny* bike ride. Mom kept the little ones home, where they snuggled before a roaring fire with a pile of picture books. The family was reunited the following weekend when we went with Doug to Dallas for CME. We stayed in a swank hotel that was apparently hosting a cheerleading convention across the hall from the medical conference. The place was *swarming*. I've never in my life seen so many pom-poms and ponytails under one roof. Our boys nearly tripped over one another volunteering to fetch ice or towels or newspapers or suitcases—*anything* that would necessitate a trip to the lobby where the teams congregated.

> *The joy of brightening other lives, bearing each others' burdens, easing other's loads and supplanting empty hearts and lives with generous gifts becomes for us the magic of Christmas.*
>
> W.C. Jones

We made our annual trek to Houston in March. Bethany stayed home alone and was sorely missed— particularly as we pedaled those six-seater surreys down Galveston Beach (her strong legs would have been an asset when the little ones tuckered out). Worried her big sister wouldn't get enough hugs and kisses while we were away, Rebekah gave her an extra helping of each before we left town. "I *love* Bethany," she told us. "In fact, sometimes I think we adopted an *angel*." We had to agree, especially when we came back from our trip to find the table spread with a delicious gourmet dinner Beth whipped up in honor of our homecoming. Some token souvenir might've been better appreciated, but the only thing we brought home from the coast was a gastro-intestinal virus which the family juggled back and forth for six long weeks. Ben, who was first to succumb, was also first to recover and rendered tender loving care when the rest of us fell ill (perhaps to assuage his guilt for sharing the bug to begin with). Our washer and dryers were kept in constant use to furnish enough fresh linens for the afflicted, as this illness generated a staggering amount of projectile vomit. Joseph set the family record for distance (which Ben documented with a digital camera before a babysitting David dutifully mopped up), but Daniel exceeded everyone in sheer volume, drenching his mother so thoroughly and often that she took to rocking him in a raincoat.

April brought colored eggs and cottontails: A pair of wrens raised six hatchlings in the watering can on our back porch. We watched with rapt attention as the little brood ate its meals, got its feathers, and learned to fly. And a rabbit family took up residence in our azalea bed, feasting on phlox blossoms all summer long. The bunnies thrived; not so, the perennials. April also brought *snow*! The flakes fell heavily on Easter weekend, but didn't stick—a good thing, considering Doug and the boys were in the middle of a 30-mile bike ride when the flurries began. True to his plan, Doug celebrated his 40th birthday by competing in the Las Colinas triathlon. In the end, he and Samuel opted to swim/bike/run the shorter Olympic distance (blame it on the three broken ribs Doug sustained during a race back in January), so David finished the Half-Ironman by himself. The open-water swim was more unnerving than any of them anticipated, although they'd been warned by seasoned tri-athletes they'd need to slather petroleum jelly on their ankles to prevent other swimmers from *grabbing hold*! Even so, all three finished the course, and nobody drowned, for which we were most grateful. Jennifer found out a few days before the race that she is indeed pregnant again, which made her feel as if she had received a stay of execution. She wasn't ready to compete, anyway, as she'd done no serious training since the onset of March's Puke-Fest. Our whole family was excited about this new baby, but none more so than Rachel, who immediately announced to her weekly kindergarten co-op that "Mommy's expecting twins!" News travels fast, so Jennifer found herself repeatedly explaining to happy inquirers that, unless Rachel knows something *we* don't know, *that* rumor is just wishful thinking.

A friend divided her bulb garden this spring and called to offer us the culls. She had canna, day lily, iris, daffodil, narcissus, liriope—a can of each—so how many could we use? Picturing a few transplants in half a dozen coffee tins, Jennifer enthusiastically told her we'd take them *all*. As it turns out, those "cans" were the 39-gallon garbage variety, stuffed to overflowing with *thousands* of bulbs. It took the better part of May to get them all in the ground, but the blooms should be spectacular next spring, naturalized along the trails through our woods. We finished in time to celebrate Isaac's birthday. He turned four, but insisted he was five, being firmly convinced that his ability to pedal a bike without training wheels entitled him to skip a year. When Mom explained that, if we added a year for riding bikes, we'd have to subtract two for wearing pull-ups, Isaac promptly changed into Spiderman briefs (which he's worn successfully ever since) and agreed to keep his thumb folded down for another twelve months when anyone asks his age.

June took us to the Pacific Northwest. We traveled 6000 miles with no speeding tickets, even though Doug did most of the driving (much of it while examining his "vacation beard" in the rearview mirror—*where did all that gray come from?*). Our route led through landscapes as varied as they were beautiful: snowcapped mountains, redwood forests, sandy beaches, sparkling rivers, and lush vineyards stretching in tidy rows over hill and dale. (We also spotted gas stations charging $4/gallon—*not* a pretty site). The kids bore well our long hours on the road. The only complaints we heard from the backseats were, "I'm starving again—give me something to eat" (from Isaac, five minutes after every meal), "Can we go to the hotel, so I can get in bed?" (also from Isaac, who *loved* the Spiderman sheets Mom made for his porta-crib), and "Pass me something to throw up in—quick!" (from just about everybody at some point along the way—we'd never have survived those tortuous mountain passes without our Dramamine and an ample supply of trash basket liners).... We hiked to St. Mary's Glacier outside Denver. The snow grew deeper as we made our way up the steep trail, so everyone was glad that Mom had insisted we wear our jackets. Besides keeping us warm, those slick nylon windbreakers were perfect for zipping down icy slopes and for building a makeshift stretcher to cart little ones back to dry land. The boys couldn't resist pelting one another with snowballs at every turn, and Samuel even *ate* several handfuls of the whitest crystals he could find, until a younger sibling demonstrated that when nature calls, it doesn't really turn snow *yellow*—it rinses it *clean*.... We enjoyed a bountiful outdoor barbecue at Yosemite Park. Isaac was "still starving" after polishing off a hot dog, lemonade, eight slices of watermelon, and at least that many s'mores (maybe he confuses feeling *starved* with feeling *stuffed*?).... We stopped along the coast in San Simeon to watch the sea lions, but were equally enthralled by a colony of ground squirrels that flocked to our feet as soon as we stepped out of the van, darting between our legs, planting their little paws on our knees and begging for a handout.... Doug ordered a round of fruit smoothies at the fancy restaurant atop Seattle's Space Needle. They were delicious, but the instant Isaac's cup hit the floor, we remembered why we normally restrict the kids to water only—the resultant explosion splattered everything within a ten-foot radius, including a table full of remarkably gracious Japanese businessmen. Had our entire family not been wearing matching shirts at the time, I'm sure the older kids would have dispersed at once and pretended not to know us.... Back home in Tyler, we got a phone call from friends vacationing in Wyoming. "Did y'all stay at the Embassy Suites in Salt Lake City a few nights ago?" they queried. It seems our big family had so impressed a little Asian couple staying at the same hotel that they were still talking about us days later, telling complete strangers at Yellowstone Park how well-behaved our children were. In fact, they provided such a detailed description (mom expecting eleventh child, oldest boy extremely tall, everyone dressed exactly alike, etc.) that our friends knew immediately it had to be us and called to let us know we'd become something of a legend. Our reaction? We were just glad that couple spied us eating *breakfast in Salt Lake* and not *lunch in Seattle*—our reputation might have been ruined!

We resumed school in July, to allow for a longer break at Christmas. It's usually the scorching heat that drives us indoors, back to our books, but this year it was torrential rains (definitely atypical of Texas summers, though we had fun kayaking in swollen streams and surfing down spillways). Our quiet Rachel turned six and officially began first grade, having already taught herself to read and write the names of everyone in the family—a feat which amazes older siblings who aren't such natural spellers.... Time came to renew the inspection stickers on all our vehicles this month, so Doug drove to TJC to trade cars with Bethany, who was working freshman orientation. Springing up the steps to the student center, he tracked her down, gave her a hug, traded keys, then left, at which point her friends came rushing over to find out who the cute guy was. "You mean my dad?" Beth seemed puzzled. "Your *dad*?" Her friends gasped, "But he looks so *young*! We thought he was your boyfriend!" I don't know how Bethany took this remark, but Doug considered it a tremendous compliment. He strutted around the house for weeks on end and worked the story into as many conversations as possible, however tangential the connection.

We celebrated our 20th anniversary in August by dusting off our old wedding video and showing it to the children. The years have been good to us. Except for a little extra padding, *neither* of us looks any different now than we did then—or so we flattered ourselves, until the kids set us straight. "Who *are* those people, anyway?" they wondered aloud. In their eyes we're ancient. Rebekah marveled that the movie was even *in color*—and had *sound*.... Daniel celebrated his second birthday this month. He's finally started to talk, which has the whole family ecstatic. Up until a month earlier, the only words he'd voice were "mom", "dad", "ball," and "bye" (and *those* very infrequently). Most of his communication was done strictly in sign language: "More milk, please!" or "Where's Daddy?" or "My diaper stinks. Change me." He lets us know he's awake in the morning, not by crying or calling, but by pushing a button to turn on his music box. As soon as we open the door to his room, he pops up with a smile, shuts off the music, and stretches out his arms to be held. Who *couldn't* love a baby like our little Diaper Dan?

We celebrated three more birthdays in September. Rebekah turned eight. She loves all things *Little House*: She names her dolls Laura, Mary, and Carrie, wears her hair in two long braids wherever she goes, and wishes her Pa would grow *his* hair long and curl it, à la Michael Landon, although Ma prefers the clean-cut style Pa normally wears. Joseph turned ten. He loves origami, computers, and gymnastics, but is also a whiz at math, earning straight 100's on all his tests and homework. Bethany turned eighteen. She stays so busy attending class, assisting in the biology lab, serving in student government, tutoring algebra and chemistry, and going to Bible study that we seldom see her at all anymore. Not only does she miss dinner and story time more evenings than not, but she was unable to accompany us on any of our road trips this year. *Bummer!* We do spot her occasionally at the track or in the pool—she, Ben, and Joe all trained consistently enough to complete their first triathlon this month, while Doug, David and Samuel finished their fourth. Bethany also attempted to revamp her mother's dowdy wardrobe this fall, so if you spot Jennifer about town looking uncharacteristically chic, now you'll know why!

Sam and Ben both had birthdays in October. At age 14, Samuel's become a formidable ping-pong opponent, consistently beating the rest of us, even when he plays left-handed. After our washing machine went on the blink this summer, Mom and Dad unwittingly helped Sam realize a lifelong dream by dropping him and Ben at the corner laundry with 25 loads of dirty clothes. When we returned later to help fold the dry stuff, Sam was psyched. "I'm *so glad* you let me do this!" he enthused sincerely, "I've *always wanted* to wash clothes at a Laundromat!" At age 12, Benjamin is a bit of an extrovert. Somewhere along the way, our chubby-cheeked preschooler who seldom spoke evolved into a lanky adolescent who seldom stops. The doorbell at our house is constantly ringing, and nine times out of ten, it is some friend of Ben's, wanting him to play. He's just as popular with younger siblings, for whom he always seems to be planning some grand adventure or preparing a tasty snack (though few share his fondness for peanut butter cookie dough, which Ben mixes without the eggs, so Dad won't freak out about salmonella poisoning—they'd much rather eat his short-order omelets, which he makes a great show of flipping in the air).... The kids were all thrilled to become aunts and uncles this month when their sister-in-law delivered a beautiful bouncing baby boy. After a *very short* labor (Jon and Matti made it to the hospital in time, but the OB didn't), Aiden Kenneth William Flanders was born October 9, a healthy 8 lbs 14 oz. He has his father's eyes, his mother's smile, and the rest of us wrapped securely around his little finger.... More good news: After 15 years and two activations, the Army declared Doug's obligation to the military fulfilled and discharged him as a lieutenant colonel on October 16. Two days later, we hit the road again, meandering our way to Cape Cod, where Doug attended a conference geared to physicians who aspire to be authors, a goal he's pursuing more aggressively having now turned forty. The trip was relaxing and pleasantly uneventful: no one got stuck in the narrow passages of Mammoth Cave (though it was a tight squeeze for an 8-month pregnant belly), nobody toppled over the rail into Niagara Falls (though Rachel tried to mount it for a better view), and none of us broke our necks on the surf simulator at Great Wolf Lodge (though Doug cracked another rib trying to traverse one pool's floating lily pads). We reinforced our early American history studies with stops in Boston, Philadelphia, DC, and Williamsburg (colonial costumes in tow).

> *Peace on earth will come to stay, When we live Christmas every day.*
>
> Helen Steiner Rice

November found us heading home, the fall foliage and a visit to Plimoth Plantation having put us in the mood to celebrate Thanksgiving with grateful hearts. Since Jennifer's impending delivery promises to make December even busier than usual, we are mailing these updates early this year. We realize folks who receive our newsletter fall into one of two basic groups: those who roll their eyes and toss it on the nightstand to be used as a remedy for insomnia (as one of Doug's partners, under the misconception that Doug writes our updates, conspiratorially confessed to Jennifer that *he* does) and those who savor every word and read it aloud to neighbors, coworkers, family, and friends (a reaction which leaves us baffled every time we hear it). If you're in the first group, you likely dozed off three pages ago. If you're in the second, you might be interested to know that we are in the process of posting all our old Christmas letters, along with photos, organization tips, and other fun stuff, on a new website, *www.flandersfamily.info,* which we plan to update monthly as an experiment in keeping in touch with extended family, distant friends, and children who've moved away from home. All this to say, if you don't want to wait until next year's update to find out whether #11 is a boy or girl, then check the site in January for birth statistics and pictures of our latest addition. Meanwhile, we pray that Christ will be exalted in our home and yours this holiday season as our hearts joyfully resound, "Thanks be unto God for His unspeakable gift." May the Lord bless and keep you in the coming year.

With love from the Flanders family:
Doug and Jennifer, Bethany, David, Samuel, Benjamin, Joseph,
Rebekah, Rachel, Isaac, Daniel, and Baby-Due-Soon

- *The Christmas Story* -

Luke 2:1-20

And it came to pass in those days, that there went out a decree from Caesar Augustus, that all the world should be taxed. (And this taxing was first made when Cyrenius was governor of Syria.) And all went to be taxed, every one into his own city. And Joseph also went up from Galilee, out of the city of Nazareth, into Judaea, unto the city of David, which is called Bethlehem; (because he was of the house and lineage of David) to be taxed with Mary his espoused wife, being great with child. And so it was, that, while they were there, the days were accomplished that she should be delivered. And she brought forth her firstborn son, and wrapped him in swaddling clothes, and laid him in a manger; because there was no room for them in the inn. And there were in the same country shepherds abiding in the field, keeping watch over their flock by night. And, lo, the angel of the Lord came upon them, and the glory of the Lord shone round about them: and they were sore afraid. And the angel said unto them, "Fear not: for, behold, I bring you good tidings of great joy, which shall be to all people. For unto you is born this day in the city of David a Saviour, which is Christ the Lord. And this shall be a sign unto you: Ye shall find the babe wrapped in swaddling clothes, lying in a manger." And suddenly, there was with the angel a multitude of the heavenly host, praising God and saying, "Glory to God in the Highest, and on earth, peace, goodwill toward man."

2008

Jennifer spent most of last December wishing "the days were accomplished that she should be delivered." Baby #11 was two weeks late. When our OB finally tried to schedule an induction, we were originally turned away because there was "no room" at the hospital. But the charge nurse took pity and, when Jennifer showed up on the doorstep in active labor, scrambled to find a bed for her. Just half an hour later, at 6:07 a.m. on December 21, our precious little Gabriel Arthur made his way into the world. At 10 lbs 6 oz, he tied Jon as our biggest baby yet, a fitting conclusion to what had also been the easiest pregnancy and quickest delivery.

Doug resolved in January to devote more time to writing. To that end, he scheduled a week off every month to work on his novel, which he could have finished by now if *life* had not kept getting in the way—but at least we got to enjoy having him at home... Not all our New Year's resolutions were so ambitious: Samuel and Benjamin determined to speak only the Queen's English this year. For five days on the trot every word out of their mouths was delivered in a distinct British accent. The lads might've kept it up, too, had Pops not thrown a spanner in the works by fubbiddin'em t'talk 'at way't chutch on Sunday.... These two also worked overtime preparing for our homeschool group's Geography Bee this month. All the practice paid off: Samuel took first place, and Ben came in second.

In celebration of David's sixteenth birthday, we hosted a father-son log-splitting competition in February. Since several of those sinewy boys now tower over their dads (including one of our own), we thought the odds might be in their favor, but mass won over muscle in the end: bigger beltlines bested bulging biceps. David laid aside his violin this year to spend more time at the piano, where long arms and large hands are more of an asset than a liability. Photography is another of his favorite pastimes: He is constantly darting out of the house with Mom's camera, tripod, and telephoto lens in hand to snap pictures of some woodland creature he's spied through his bedroom window. He's captured some stunning images of birds, bunnies, toads, turtles, raccoons, one very long (non-venomous) rat snake and also—much to our surprise—a whitetail deer that came to nibble on the grass we laid behind the tree house this spring.

March 1 found our entire family donning spandex suits to take "before" photos (we won't be publishing *those* on our website) prior to starting P90-X, a rigorous workout regimen that promised to whip us into shape in just three months. Enthusiasm ran high. The master bedroom was transformed into an aerobics class as young and old alike lined up every night before dinner for calisthenics, plyometrics, and kempo karate. We lasted almost two weeks before we ran out of steam, which means that those of us who didn't already *have* a "beach body" didn't *get one* in time for our trip to Hilton Head this summer... Doug's folks came to visit the end of the month. We took them to Caldwell Zoo, Goodman Museum, and the Azalea Trails, where we discovered the world's best lemonade stand (fresh-squeezed!) on the corner of College and Shaw. Grandma and Grandpa stayed six days (at our *house,* not at the lemonade stand), but managed to escape without catching the stomach virus our little ones were passing around at the time.

Doug drove David, Samuel, and a vanload of teenagers to the state capital in April for a weeklong hands-on government practicum. They loved getting to participate in mock legislative sessions held in the actual House Chamber. Too young for TeenPact, Ben and Joe stayed here and helped Mom hold the fort at home…. April brought glad tidings to Bethany: She was named "TJC Tutor of the Month," was offered a summer job working for Pine Cove at Crier Creek as a life guard and family camp counselor (which she accepted), and was chosen to participate in a physics program hosted by NASA (which she declined, since it conflicted with an honor society convention in Philadelphia). The only thing that would've made her month any better would be getting her acceptance letter to Texas A&M, but she waited on pins and needles another six weeks before *that* good news arrived.

Isaac turned five in May. He wanted cobbler instead of cake for his birthday, so we all grabbed our buckets and hiked through the woods gathering juicy wild blackberries. Mmmm! They were delicious, and the timing was perfect: When we returned to harvest more the following week, there was not a berry to be found. In honor of being such a big boy now (he's almost caught up to Rachel in height), Isaac was given a place at the table for our family Spoons tournament. Now Daniel alone must serve as Game Marshal, making sure there are "no shifty eyes, no twitchy fingers." Spoons provides good character training for our little ones, who are all such *serious* players. They get so focused on their cards that they forget to watch the spoons, and it takes a great deal of self-control for them to quell their disappointment when they lose. The older ones sympathize (and sometimes slide them a spoon so they can stay in the game), because they're learning the same lesson themselves shooting hoops. Every night after dinner, they line up on the driveway with Dad for a quick round of Knock-Out. Learning to win graciously and to lose with dignity has sure taken a lot of practice! Anyone who fails to control his (or her) temper during the competition gets invited to be Guest Speaker at Bible time afterward and read aloud selected passages from *Proverbs for Parenting*, a topical arrangement of Scripture under such headings as anger, pride, patience, and humility. (Sad to say, even Mom and Dad have had to take occasional turns reading choice verses). The nightly games of Knock-Out ended once the pool opened, which conveniently coincided with Doug's finally *winning* a round (and establishing a new rule that, thenceforth, all losers must greet the victor by crying, "Hail to the Champion"). Then it was on to new things: Rachel, Isaac, and Daniel learned to swim this summer under the expert tutelage of their beloved sister-in-law, who is also a certified swim instructor. While Matti worked with the little ones, the big ones tried to outdo one another performing tricks off the diving boards. Even Mom learned to do a back flip, thanks to the enthusiastic coaching she received from Dad and the boys. She'd do about three flips a night (to prove she wasn't chicken), then would spend the rest of lesson time poolside, lounging with our grandbaby in her lap. With his sun-bleached hair, bright blue eyes, and golden tan, Aiden looks as if he were *born* wearing a swim diaper—and he's every bit as happy *in* the water as he is out of it.

Sweet Rachel turned seven in June. She's as quiet as a mouse, but full of surprises. Would you have guessed, for instance, that Rachel can do more *chin-ups* than almost anyone else in our family? In perfect form, too, which is why we've started calling her "Muscle Girl." She brushes her teeth eight times a day and would take as many showers if we didn't draw the line at two or three. Rachel loves to read, read, read—and you should hear her quote Scripture! Loud and clear, without a hint of timidity. She and Isaac were both baptized this summer as testimony to their faith in God…. Gabriel learned to *crawl* this month, so now there's no stopping him. He's a happy boy, with a habit of sucking on his upper lip that gives him an adorably elfish grin, wide enough to accommodate all ten fingers at once. He enjoys being outdoors, especially if it means being strapped in the baby seat on back of Mom's bike. Jennifer took the kids to Mesquite for the Rodeo Ride this month, and Gabriel slept contently through the entire thing, including a spill Mom took while trying to coax our preschooler to pedal *a little faster* (even after Isaac stopped riding his brakes, we averaged only 2 ½ mph, making us grateful we'd taken the five-mile route). Samuel pumped Daniel and supervised Rachel; David kept up with

Rebekah and Joseph; and Benjamin served as a liaison between tortoises and hares, even jogging back after he'd finished the course to push Isaac up that last long hill. It was fun, but we missed Dad, who was on call that weekend and unable to join us…. Jonathan's growing family moved into a new rent house this month after a finicky septic system rendered their duplex uninhabitable (in Matti's opinion, at least, who's expecting our *second* grandbaby and must appease a hypersensitive nose whenever she's pregnant). Jon also switched employers this year, having found a job with better hours and higher pay working as a pharmacy tech. He's still taking classes at TJC part time, slowly but surely knocking out his pre-med requirements.

Beth completed her duties at Crier Creek in July and flew to Hilton Head to meet the rest of us for a week of biking, beach combing, kayaking, and consuming crab legs, clam chowder, and key lime pie. Since Bethany would be leaving for college shortly after our return home, Jennifer was determined to take our Christmas picture while we were all together. This was easier said than done. Glaring sunlight, low batteries, cranky babies, and background bikinis conspired against our getting a decent shot. Consequently, every time we turned around, Mom was re-dressing us in our not-so-white shirts and khaki shorts ("Don't worry, nobody will be able to *smell* them in the picture!") and dragging us back to the beach for yet another attempt. She finally thought to pray for God's blessing before the *third* photo shoot and was granted success, at last. I'll bet you can't even tell by looking that one of us has his shirt on backwards—to hide all the ketchup stains on front.

Motivated by the book *Do Hard Things*, David and Samuel spent the rest of their summer racking up college credits by taking CLEP exams. They've already tested out of college algebra and psychology, and are now studying for pre-calculus and freshman composition…. Daniel turned three in August. He is the spittin' image of brother Isaac, especially when both are dressed in their matching Spiderman costumes. Even *we* had trouble telling them apart before Isaac gave himself a burr recently (*he* started the haircut; *Mom* finished it). Daniel's partner Benjmin sees that he is dressed as neat as a pin whenever we go out— hair combed and parted, shirttail tucked in, socks and shoes on the appropriate feet— but invariably Daniel's clothes are on inside out and backwards by the time we reach our destination, since he prefers to dress himself and insists on practicing constantly.

Dad, David, and Samuel signed up for scuba diving lessons in September. They found it unnerving to take their final exam in a murky lake thirty feet below the surface where they could scarcely see their hand in front of their face, but all three passed the course and are dreaming of their next undersea adventure, preferably in the crystal clear waters of the Caribbean…. Our vibrant Rebekah turned nine on the ninth. She loves horses, full skirts, and cowboy boots, and has recently learned to quilt, crochet, and play the harmonica. Joe turned eleven on the eleventh. He is into astronomy, math, botany, and Bionicles, though not necessarily in that order. He and Rebekah both got road bikes this year and now ride to breakfast on Saturday mornings with their dad and older brothers. All six wear matching jerseys and call themselves *Team Molasses* (they're slow but sweet). Those who aren't slow-of-necessity are slow-by-choice, making sure no stragglers get left behind (besides, if they leave Dad in the dust, who'll pay for their pancakes?).... Doug volunteered Jennifer to paint a street market mural on the wall of Gilbert's El Charro this month. About 90% of the work had been done by someone else over a year ago, but progress had obviously come to a standstill. Seeing this, Doug summoned the manager to our table. "My wife is *an artist*," he told the man authoritatively, "and she'd be happy to finish your mural in the style it was begun." The manager called the owner, who smiled at Jennifer but directed his questions to Doug. "How much she charge?" he wanted to know. Doug told him she'd do the work for free—if he liked it, he could buy our lunch. So he agreed, Jennifer finished the painting, the kids helped her do it, and our entire family feasted on free fajitas from one of our favorite local restaurants. When Jennifer later ribbed Doug about calling her *an artist*, he defended himself. "What did you expect me to say? My wife is OCD... and those pencil marks are driving her crazy?" (He was kidding, of course. It was the *gesso* that messed with her mind). The children did such a good job on that little project that Mom put them to work painting another mural at home. Next time you're here, you'll have to check out all the blossoms and birdhouses that now adorn the wall of our classroom bath.

Samuel turned fifteen in October. Except for playing the piano and ultimate Frisbee, Sam does just about everything one-handed, including gathering trash, watering ferns, mixing orange juice, and fetching mail. That's because the other arm is usually supporting Gabriel on his hip, which is where his little brother begs to be most of the time. *Everyone* loves to hold the baby when he's happy, but Samuel's willing to tote him around when he's cranky, too.... Benjamin turned thirteen this month. He is all about house plans, whether it's drawing blueprints with his new drafting set, sketching elevations with colored pencils (one of his drawings won first place at the fair), designing dream homes with *Lego Creator,* or pouring over the latest issue of *Tyler's Home and Land Guide.* Ben also has a knack for winning stuffed animals out of those "electronic claw" machines. We've even seen him pull out three at a time on a single quarter, easy as pie.... David and Samuel spent a week at World View Academy this month, stopping in College Station on the way to visit their sister. We all miss Bethany terribly, but I think she misses us even more. After living eighteen years amid the hustle-bustle of our active brood, her little townhouse must seem deafeningly quiet, even if her roommate *is* a like-minded Christian who loves to talk.... We pitched our tents and spent the second week of October camping out in Big Sandy, surrounded by homeschool families as big as our own. It was delightful. The fellowship warmed our hearts, and the campfires warmed our toes. Brr! Those nights were chilly! Dad and David struck camp early to catch a train to Illinois for the Chicago Marathon. David finished the race in under five hours; Doug didn't finish at all. He was so stiff from sleeping on the train that he barely made it past the start line before throwing in the towel and heading to the breakfast buffet and, after that, the Runner's Expo. That's where he bought our new bathroom scale, which analyzes every limb of your body for muscle mass, bone weight, and body fat composition, then assigns a physiological age based on those readings. It told Doug that he has the body of a thirty-something, so he naturally brought it home. Jennifer wishes he hadn't; she was happier not knowing that *her body* belongs in a nursing home.

No doubt inspired by the speed with which his little nephew is getting around these days, Gabriel took his first steps in November. His healthy development is just one of countless blessings for which we offer thanks this season. We live in changing times, but Jesus Christ is the same yesterday, today, and forever. For that, we are especially grateful.

We hope your family has a very merry Christmas and a fruitful New Year. May God keep us all in His tender care and may Christ reign in our hearts, come what may.

With love from the Flanders family:
Doug and Jennifer, Bethany, David, Samuel, Benjamin, Joseph,
Rebekah, Rachel, Isaac, Daniel, and Gabriel

2009

A stomach virus knocked our whole family out of commission last December, forcing us to miss all the holiday parties, Christmas pageants, and family celebrations that we normally attend. It takes a while for any bug to work its way through a household our size, but this one cycled through two and a half times before we were finally rid of it. Our health was restored by New Year's Eve, so we were able to join friends for fireworks, volleyball, and several rounds of "the hat game," which quickly became a new family favorite (players put words or phrases in a hat, then take turns guessing who wrote what).

Doug surprised us on January 1st by tearing up his standard list of resolutions—to exercise more and to give up all things fried or caffeinated—in order to focus his full attention on a single goal this year: WRITE THE BOOK! He asked Jennifer to make a "Write the Book!" sign for the bulletin board in his closet, but she went the extra mile and also printed "Write the Book!" labels to stick on his phones and beeper, laminated "Write the Book!" cards to post near sinks and showers, and even painted "Write the Book!" on our bedroom ceiling using invisible, glow-in-the-dark paint. The extra encouragement seemed to work, and Doug churned out pages left and right. When he started grinding his teeth by night and grumping at the kids by day, however, Jennifer feared she'd gone too far. Happily, equilibrium was restored once she washed "Write the Book!" off all our message boards, stopped tucking "Write the Book!" reminders into the pockets of his scrubs, and left off penning "Write the Book!" on every tenth sheet of toilet paper. Less stressed, Doug progressed at a slower but steady and sustainable clip, with plenty of time left over to relax and spend with the family, including a second grandson, Sawyer Ethan, whom Matti delivered December 29 at a whopping 9 lbs 10 oz—the sweetest little thumb-sucker you could ever hope to meet.

David turned seventeen in February and bought his first pair of Five Fingers, thus taking his father's penchant for funky footwear to a whole new level. Six foot six-and-a-half inches, he still enjoys competing in triathlon and spent the summer training his little sisters to

Our Favorite Christmas Stories to Read Aloud

Luke 2:1-20
(King James Version)

The Best
Christmas Pageant Ever
(Barbara Robinson)

A Christmas Carol
(Charles Dickens)

The Year of the Perfect
Christmas Tree
(Gloria Houston)

The Gift of the Magi
(O. Henry)

Who Is Coming to Our House?
(Joseph Slate)

How the Grinch Stole Christmas
(Dr. Seuss)

The First Night
(B.G. Hennessey)

Family Devotions for the
Advent Season
(James L. Evans)

The Night Before Christmas
(Clement C. Moore)

Good Tidings
(Our Family Christmas Letters)

do the same. After finding a widget for his Mac that allows him to scan barcodes, he used it to catalogue our entire home library—all 3922 volumes, not including duplicates. When Benjamin heard the final count, he observed, "Wow! Just eighty-eight more books, and we'd have an even four thousand." "You mean *seventy*-eight, don't you, Son?" Dad corrected, "We only need *seventy*-eight more books to make four thousand." Our quick-witted Ben never missed a beat, "Well, I was trying to say that with eighty-eight more books we'd have an even four thousand *ten*, but you cut me off before I could finish."

We tackled our biggest spring project yet in March. After getting an unbelievably low quote from a local nursery on buying St. Augustine sod in bulk, Doug decided to grass in almost every square inch of our land. He bought seven dumper truckloads of topsoil, compost, and hardwood mulch, which the big boys worked into the ground using a rented rototiller and a front-end loader. Meanwhile, Jennifer took a can of orange spray paint and marked borders for a dozen new flowerbeds in the shadiest areas of the yard, which our little ones then carefully outlined with three tons of river rocks. Everybody helped with the grass. We finished laying forty of the forty-four pallets we purchased before the nursery owner realized he had miscalculated. He called Doug in a panic to explain that instead of *making* thirty dollars per pallet as he'd intended, he was actually *losing* thirty! Doug assured him that it was not his intention to rob anybody, and that a good name is more important to our family than a good deal. They renegotiated, and Doug wrote him a check the same day to cover his loss and give him a modest profit. The man was so grateful that he offered us—at cost—as many shrubs and ferns as we could use. Between those and the bulbs and perennials in our front beds that needed dividing, plus miscellaneous culls from friends, our back beds took shape in short order. In the end, we were glad about the mix-up. We would likely have decided against undertaking such an ambitious landscaping project had we known upfront how much it would really cost, but we've thoroughly enjoyed the finished results, which turned out even more beautiful than we had imagined.

A cough Daniel developed in mid-February had turned into pneumonia by April. Two rounds of antibiotics cleared his lungs, but still the cough persisted. We spent the following seven months consulting specialists (ENT, allergist, pediatric pulmonologist), tweaking his diet (no more dairy), X-raying his lungs (healthy), scoping his sinuses (slightly enlarged adenoids), and screening for swine flu, strep, and TB (all negative). By the end of the summer, his prescribed daily meds had multiplied to fill an entire shelf of our bathroom cabinet. Fortunately, he was good about taking all of them. In fact, Daniel's a cooperative little patient, in general. When one physician asked Doug whether Daniel would need to be sedated for a CAT scan he'd ordered, Doug answered, "Not this kid. This kid is *great*. He won't give you a bit of trouble, will you, Daniel?" Daniel solemnly shook his head. True to his word, he lay unflinchingly still for the scan, belly down with his chin propped on a pillow, never even batting an eyelash. The techs were amazed and wanted to know Dad's secret. "No secret," Doug shrugged, "he's just a really sweet boy, aren't you, Daniel?" Daniel just smiled.

David, Samuel, and Benjamin hit the road in May, headed to Tennessee (alone!) for TeenPact National Convention. Emboldened by the fact that David had been elected Governor of Texas TeenPact a month earlier, all three ran for office at the convention, so their Tahoe was consequently crammed full with extremely creative campaign materials. David and Benjamin were running mates on the presidential ticket, while Samuel vied for a seat in the senate. Alas, none of them made it out of the primaries (but all are already planning to try again next year). They fared better playing Ultimate Frisbee, where their team made it to the quarterfinals. When they got back home, David was elected president and Samuel second vice-president of the TACHE Class of 2010. Isaac turned six this month. He has grown over three inches since his last birthday, but Rachel has managed to stay just a hair ahead of him, to her relief and his chagrin. Our middle ones played soccer this spring, Joe and Rebekah enjoyed it, but Isaac and Rachel seemed more interested in digging in the dirt and making clover chains on the sidelines than in chasing a ball across the field. Their sporting tastes run more to "Zombie Tree Tag," a game the kids made up themselves and our whole family spent countless summer evenings playing in that plush new grass that now grows under the trees beyond our fence. The game's a blast (you'll find rules for play posted on our family website).

June brought Bethany home for the summer. She is loving life in College Station, attending a wonderful church, making lots of sweet friends, and enjoying her classes—including *Genes, Ecology, and Evolution,* where such scant evidence was offered to support evolution's claims that the course actually affirmed rather than shook her faith, and *Organic Chemistry*, where she did so well that A&M hired her to teach supplemental instruction classes for students taking *O Chem* this fall. Having lately discovered a talent for writing music, Bethany spent a large portion of her break hammering out new songs at our piano with tunes so catchy the rest of us ended up humming them for weeks on end. Several of Beth's school friends drove up to visit us over the course of the summer, among them a 6'9" pre-med student who had been friendly enough over the past several months to make us wonder whether he might be coming to have a little talk with Doug. We were grossly mistaken, as evidenced by the fact that he tried to cajole Bethany into setting him up with one of her friends while he was here! The silver lining? David's status as the tallest guy in our family is momentarily secure (he was sweating the threat more than he likes to admit), and Beth subsequently wrote her best song yet, "Antithesis of Bitterness" (which you can hear—you guessed it—on our family website).

July was filled with typical summer fare—story times at the public library, trips to area museums, blueberry picking, CLEP prep, and lots of pleasure reading. Mom insisted that anyone too old for naps must read quietly for an hour each afternoon while babies slept. Most of our kids counted the minutes until they were free to go back outdoors and play, but Rachel would often stay in the library until dinnertime, soaking up chapter after chapter. Samuel, too, spent much of the summer with his nose in a book. Although he has traditionally preferred to read science and history, when he missed passing his College Composition CLEP by two points last January because he ran out of time on the reading comprehension portion, Doug prescribed a

> *Christmas is the season for kindling the fire of hospitality in the hall, the genial flame of charity in the heart.*
>
> Washington Irving

steady diet of fiction to increase his speed. He knew what Sam needed most was to get so drawn into a book that he couldn't put it down, something not likely to happen with all the non-fiction he'd been reading. Doug assigned the first few titles himself—a little Louis L'Amour followed by some Lloyd Alexander—after which Samuel was allowed to pick his own. The strategy worked. When he retook the CLEP (after the requisite six month waiting period and with no further study), Sam passed with flying colors, scoring a full 12 points higher than on his first attempt. In the interim, he developed a deeper appreciation for the valuable lessons to be learned through narrative storytelling—even Jesus knew that well-spun tales about a good Samaritan, a house on the rock, or an ungrateful slave would resonate with His listeners and stick with them far longer than simple admonitions to show compassion, make wise choices, or forgive offenders.

Doug's determination to "Write the Book!" had begun to lag by August, but if the residual "Write the Book!" signs still posted around our house failed to motivate him, Jennifer found something else that certainly did the trick: *She* finished writing *her* book! It took two and a half years to research and write the first half of this marriage manual, but only four months to finish the second half, due primarily to the fact she had lots of friends praying for the project by then and a thirty-one pound alarm clock named Gabriel who faithfully woke her up at 2:48 AM all summer long, which is when she did the bulk of her writing. The book was complete by our 22nd wedding anniversary, so we dropped the manuscript in the mail on our way to celebrate. We had further cause for rejoicing this month when we learned that Jennifer is pregnant again. We surprised the children by announcing the news while playing the hat game. Dad had the hat, but only pretended to read what the kids had written. Instead, he substituted phrases like "Great Expectations," "Is everybody here?" "Cheaper by the Dozen," "I know a secret—but don't tell anyone," "Babies are so sweet," "Morning sickness," "We need a Nathan," "Could it be twins?" "1 + 1 = 12," and—what finally gave it away—"The rabbit died." The revelation elicited squeals of delight, hugs all around, and inquiries as to how Mom is feeling. Answer: *Absolutely terrific and abundantly blessed!!*

By September, we found ourselves caught up in a virtual whirlwind of activity. School was back in full swing; Joe and Rebekah took piano and (with Ben) ballroom dance lessons; Jennifer attended weekly chorus rehearsals after successfully auditioning for the ETSO's upcoming performance of Handel's *Messiah*; Rachel joined Rebekah's *Bright Lights* Bible study group; David and Samuel spent Tuesdays and Thursdays taking biology and chemistry at TJC; and Matti (now expecting our *third* grandbaby) came over two afternoons a week to cook with Jennifer. Preparing meals in bulk helped keep our family going during the hectic days ahead: In the course of six weeks, we celebrated six family birthdays, spent eight days at family camp, competed in one triathlon (David) and a half-marathon (David and Ben), and hosted over 400 guests between a Class of 2010 Bunco party, a bridal shower, Samuel's surprise 16th birthday party, and an outdoor wedding. And if that weren't enough to keep us busy, we also tackled a lengthy list of home improvement projects that (Doug thought) needed attention before the wedding: we spread another fifty bales of pine straw along the trails through our woods, pruned countless sucker limbs and low-hanging branches from all our trees, got rid of eight racing bikes and our massive, much-loved swing-set/fort (unbeknownst to Mom and the kids, who were fairly shocked to find strangers in our yard dismantling the thing), refinished all the patio furniture (which Jennifer did herself, to keep her compulsive husband from carting it to Goodwill), resurfaced the back porch, and touched up the paint on the baseboards in our kitchen (which barely had time to dry before the bridal march began).

> *It comes every year*
> *and will go on forever.*
> *And along with Christmas*
> *belong the keepsakes and the*
> *customs. Those humble,*
> *everyday things*
> *a mother clings to, and ponders,*
> *like Mary in the secret spaces*
> *of her heart.*
>
> Marjorie Holmes

Doug finally finished the first draft of his novel in October. Hooray! A friend of ours owns the cabin in which Earnest Hemingway wrote the closing chapters of *A Farewell to Arms,* and Doug had considered flying to Wyoming to pen the final pages of *The Prodigy Project* sitting in the same chair, at the same desk. Instead, he ended up typing at least one of those chapters on a laptop, at a picnic table, during a campout, between family bike rides, volleyball games, heavy rainstorms, and marshmallow roasts. It was the perfect setting, really, for wrapping up a book about a spy with a bunch of kids who drags his unsuspecting family around the world with him while he works. Doug tried to stick with writing what he knows, so the spy is also a Christian, anesthesiologist, army reservist, and homeschooler. To our knowledge, Doug has never worked for the CIA, so that part is made up—we *think*. The story is brilliant, and Jennifer and the kids are already eagerly awaiting the sequel.

November marked the end of an era for David and Samuel: no more dragging out of bed at 6:00 a.m. to do math with Mom, since both boys passed their Calculus CLEP the end

of October. Although they won't officially graduate until May, they've effectively finished the last formal class they'll have at home; they're scheduled to take all their spring semester subjects as dual-credit courses at Tyler Junior College. They're liable to run into their big brother on campus; Jonathan is still attending TJC a couple of mornings a week, chipping away at those pre-med requirements while working full time at the pharmacy to support his growing family. Jennifer continues to stagger wake-up times for the rest of the kids: Ben now gets the earliest slot of the day, then Joe, then Rebekah and Rachel, allowing them to knock out their hardest subjects before the babies begin to stir. At least, that's how it worked before daylight saving time ended. Gabriel now insists on joining us for those pre-dawn sessions. Ughh! Joseph has been especially motivated to finish his lessons early—he landed his first job

this month, walking a neighbor's dog every day after school. He makes a point to walk it past our house, so his siblings get a chance to pet and play with Buckwheat, too. Mom and Dad love this arrangement—all the pleasures of dog-ownership and none of the responsibility—sort of like having grandkids!

That brings us back to December: Little Gabbers turns *two* this month, can you believe it? He got his first goose egg a few weeks ago after toppling out of his sister's bedroom window and smacking his head on the bricks below. Ouch! The little monkey mimics everything he sees now. We made the mistake of letting him watch the *Evian* roller-baby commercial on YouTube this fall, and he's been trying to break-dance ever since. He also loves to imitate his mama's singing and can match pitch pretty accurately, provided she hums only two or three notes at a time. Staying in tune for those longer hymns at church is more of a challenge, but he gives it his best effort: Gabriel's joyful noise can be heard over the entire congregation during Sunday morning worship services. As we celebrate the birth of our

- Jennifer Flanders -

Savior, we hope a song of praise to God and gratitude for His provision will be on your lips, as well. May the risen Lord Jesus be exalted in all our hearts and homes this holiday season and throughout the coming New Year. We wish you a Merry Christmas. Please write soon!

With love from the Flanders family:
Doug and Jennifer, Bethany, David, Samuel, Benjamin, Joseph,
Rebekah, Rachel, Isaac, Daniel, Gabriel, and Baby-Boo

Photo by Greg Mitchell

2010

     In what is becoming an annual Christmas tradition, our family spent another December holed up at home after an inadvertent exposure to chicken pox forced us into an eight-week quarantine last year. Five of the nine-kids-still-in-the-nest broke out in spots, despite the fact that all but the baby had been previously vaccinated against them. Gabriel was hardest hit—even his pox had pox—but the older boys tied for a close second. David came out of the ordeal with a thick beard, as a chin covered in crops gave him all the excuse he needed to swear off shaving for the weeks we were shut-in. The normal hustle-bustle of the holiday season completely bypassed us again, although we did venture out one night to watch *A Christmas Carol* at the local drive-in. Our kids were so grateful to get out of the house, they just snuggled together in back of the truck and didn't complain about the cold *or* the itching.

     Bethany spent an uneventful winter break on lockdown with the rest of us. She taught Mom how to use Facebook while she was home and even set up a Flanders Family "Fan Page." Nevertheless, I think she was relieved when it finally came time to return to College Station in January.... Samuel got his driver's license this month. Now David has help chauffeuring siblings about town and making eleventh-hour runs to the grocery store, but when it's time for school, the boys normally just ride their bikes and leave the Tahoe at home. They took a full load of dual-credit courses at Tyler Junior College before graduating high school this spring and transferring to UT Tyler, where they continued to compete for the top grade in all their summer school classes. Samuel was named "TJC Chemistry Student of the Year" after besting his big brother by a single point on the final. On another particularly difficult Anatomy & Physiology exam, David earned the first raw hundred his professor had awarded in over 25 years of teaching.

February brought snow, snow, and more snow, which the kids used to erect an enormous, nine-foot snowman that weighed more than all of them put together. The colossus remained standing long after the rest of the snow had melted, a testament to dogged determination, clever engineering, and brute strength.... Jennifer's new book, *Love Your Husband/Love Yourself*, was released just in time for Valentine's Day, and she had her first book signing this month at The Scroll here in Tyler. She was a little nervous that customers might avoid eye contact or veer to the opposite side of the store when they spotted her table, but was pleasantly surprised by the warm reception she received. There was even a (short) line of customers waiting for her when she arrived. She sold 22 books in three hours—one of them to a complete stranger, even! Sales picked up a few weeks later when Nancy Campbell of *Above Rubies* discovered the book and began promoting it at all her women's retreats (and ordering in lots of 100).

March took us to Dallas for a medical conference, a visit with Nana, and a little fine dining. We took the kids to The Melting Pot, and they loved it—especially the chocolate fondue strawberries, which Rebekah and Rachel have since learned to make at home for a fraction of the cost.... Our big boys attended a formal banquet this month, and parents were invited, too. It was the first time Doug has donned a tuxedo since Jennifer's sister got married twenty years ago. He opted to purchase rather than rent, in anticipation of needing one every couple of years or so now that our kids have begun to reach marriageable age. We've no weddings in the works at the moment, but as Edna Mode would say, "Luck favors the prepared!"

Abigail Rose joined our family on April 20, the day before her mother turned 45. At 10 lbs 8 oz and 22¾ inches, she set a new family record for both weight and length. We considered naming her "Abigella Varicella" in memory of the months our family spent battling chicken pox and shingles this pregnancy, but we're glad now that we opted against it. Gabriel immediately dubbed her "Baby Rose," which is a nicer nickname than "Abby McScabby" would've been and sounds especially sweet when Gabbers says it. Of course, there's something intrinsically irresistible about everything our cheerful little two-year old says. He has trouble differentiating the question "How are you?" from "How old are you?", so he flashes a thumbs-up and a peace sign at everyone he meets and answers both inquiries before they can

> *There is no ideal Christmas; only the one Christmas you decide to make as a reflection of your values, desires, affections, traditions.*
>
> Bill McKibben

even ask: "Me good. Me two." He wakes up bright and early each day and comes trotting down the hall with a pat, pat, pat of his little feet (except when he tiptoes). "Morning, Mommy," he chimes, "Me happy! You happy?" At which point Jennifer whisks him into her arms and replies heartily, "I am *now*!"

Isaac turned seven in May. He learned to do front and back flips off the diving board this summer and lost five teeth in a single week, but we think that was just a coincidence. Between the snaggle-tooth smile, his wiry cowlick, and the smattering of freckles across the bridge of his nose, he closely resembles Alfalfa of *Little Rascals* fame and acts like him, too. There are about 1001 things Isaac would rather do than sit still, unless he's parked in front of a computer, in which case he could remain motionless for the duration. It's a good thing Dad restricts him to 15 minutes of screen time a week…. Jonathan's wife, Matti, delivered our third grandson, Benjamin Chase, on May 28. He was their biggest boy yet—10 lbs 7 oz of pure sweetness—and it didn't take long for him to catch and pass his Aunt Abby in weight. Per usual, they had their baby on a reliable schedule much sooner than we did ours. Abigail slept great at night, but nary a wink while the sun was up unless cradled in her mother's arms. This stalled Jennifer's progress on most of her summer projects. There's just no good way to trim hedges and nurse a baby at the same time. Multi-tasking has its limits. Doug was invited to speak in June at a Father's Day breakfast for the senior living center where our boys regularly volunteer. He talked about how children need their dad's provision, protection, presence, and pride. *Patience* would've made a nice addition to the list, but since many of the attendees had rather short attention spans, it probably would've tried *theirs* for Doug to include anything more…. Rachel turned nine this month. She is still very quiet, although the mischievous sparkle in her eye has become more pronounced with age. She has a dry sense of humor, cracking us up with original riddles and brainteasers. She also has a competitive streak, which invariably surfaces anytime there is vertical climbing or mental math involved…. Jennifer received her first negative review this month, although it wasn't so much an evaluation of her book as it was a rant against her husband. The critic disparaged Doug's character, his profession, *and* his appearance. Not only did she give the book just one star (which, according to Amazon, means "I hated it"), but she even tried (unsuccessfully) to convince a reviewer who had given it five stars to lower her rating! Who'd have thought that a little book about *love* could stir up that much animosity?

David sliced his foot open at the pool in July and had to have six stitches, which Doug put in at home. Three of our kids were taking Anatomy & Physiology at the time, so we discussed the possibility of using this as a "see one, do one, teach one" opportunity, but since our resident physician was out of local anesthetic and unable to numb the area before suturing, David insisted we get it over with as quickly as possible…. When Rebekah found out Chick-fil-A gives free food to any customer who comes dressed as a cow on the second Friday in July (a.k.a. "Cow Appreciation Day"), she stayed up late making costumes for our entire family. Of course, David's crutches would have ruined the effect entirely, so while the rest of us dressed like a herd of Holsteins, he went as a cowboy who'd been trampled in a stampede. The costumes were a hit: The manager told us to order whatever we liked and wouldn't let us pay for a thing…. One of our neighbors hired Ben to clean their pool while they were on vacation this summer and gave our family permission to swim there while they were gone, which we gladly did. Benjamin even staged a mini-triathlon for his younger siblings, complete with goody bags and "medals" for all participants. They biked two laps around our circle drive, jogged up the hill, and then swam across the neighbors' pool. Daniel won, despite the fact he'd only been riding without training wheels and swimming without a lifejacket for a few weeks.

We celebrated our twenty-third wedding anniversary in August. Jennifer has always credited the success of our marriage to God's unfathomable grace, plus lots of love and prayers, but she overheard Doug confiding to our young neighbor, Nick Neal, that "the *real* secret to a great marriage is marrying someone super-awesome, like *Mrs. Flanders…* did." Ha! Doubtless, that helps too! Nick spent so much time at our house this summer that we unofficially adopted him as our thirteenth child. Mom even assigned him chores, which he did faithfully and cheerfully until school started and he moved back across the street to study. (If only we could get him to take his shoes and socks home, too!) Bethany finished her Bachelor's in biology and graduated magna cum laude from Texas A&M this summer. Whoop! She spent the fall semester tutoring her younger siblings in chemistry and zoology and preparing for the DAT, which she'll take in December before applying to dental school next summer. Meanwhile, she's scheduled to spend the first six months of 2011 in South Asia working with special needs children in the foothills of the Himalayas. How cool is *that*?

> *Q: Why does Scrooge love Rudolph the Red-Nosed Reindeer?*
>
> *A: Because every buck is dear to him*

For a family who doesn't keep pets, we've had all sorts of animal-interaction this year. The doe in our woods returned this spring, bringing a buck and a fawn with her. In addition to (or possibly because of) the burgeoning population of squirrels, birds, and lizards that inhabit our land, a red-tailed hawk has begun standing sentinel atop our fence post every morning. And a bright-eyed raccoon shows up nightly to nibble the bedtime snacks our kids leave on the porch for him. He drinks milk from a cup and is especially fond of licorice and peanut butter. Joseph expanded his dog-walking business this summer: By the time he celebrated his 13th birthday in September, he was walking six miles a day and getting paid good money to do it. This has allowed him to save for the future while still being generous in the present. He loves to lead his younger siblings on bike excursions to the pizza parlor, the pet shop, or the corner gas station, where he often treats them to Twizzlers and Icees. Joseph attended his first real dance this fall. His older brothers coached him beforehand on the proper way to request the pleasure of a lady's company on the dance floor. "What if she turns me down?" Joe wanted to know. "Don't worry," they assured him, "it's *never* the first one you ask." But it was! The very first girl at the very first dance! Joe just swallowed his disappointment and bravely asked another, who graciously accepted.... Rebekah turned eleven this month. She loves to bake as much as she loves to read, so she spends a good deal of time pouring over Mom's cookbooks and has become, among other things, "an accomplished maker of pancakes." Her cranberry-walnut short stacks are absolutely scrumptious—and the blueberry ones aren't bad, either. She has also learned that it's more fun to make a mess in the kitchen than to clean it up. After a year of KP duty, she recently confessed that she isn't "very fond of loading the dishwasher" and is counting the days until we change chores in December. We'll soon see if she likes doing laundry any better!

Although it meant missing the first day of Family Camp, Ben was determined to run Tyler's annual half-marathon again this October, just as he's done every year since it started. He imagines that someday they may even interview him: "Benjamin Flanders, age 97, is here today running the Tyler Half for the hundredth time." Sam's not so sure. "*Really?* You'll be 97 and running for the hundredth time?" he teased. "Of course not," Ben admitted, "I'll be 112—but I'll only *look* 97." David ran, too, and finished ahead of his younger brother who by mile eight had come to regret skipping the porta-potty station at the starting block, long line or no....

That novel Doug finished writing last fall? We are happy to announce that, after an additional twelve months of edits and revisions, *The Prodigy Project* was finally released in November and is now available in both Kindle and print editions through Amazon. Next he'll write the screenplay, as the storyline will make a blockbuster movie—something along the lines of *James Bond* meets *Cheaper By the Dozen*.... Doug also finished leading a Bible study this month based on David Platt's book *Radical,* which was the most challenging book we've read all year, if not the most controversial. About thirty friends came to our house every Thursday evening for eight weeks to brainstorm: How can we most effectively share the radical love of Jesus with those who don't know Him? We're praying God will give us wisdom and boldness as we seek to do that very thing in the months and years ahead.... Our family was blessed to have a young Chinese student named Yulong stay with us over Thanksgiving break. We took him to the zoo, the science museum, two church services, our kids' choir concert, a harvest dance, a Thanksgiving potluck, and a 5K Turkey Trot, which he finished in 23 minutes, just seconds behind David and Benjamin. We also shared meals, rode bikes, shot hoops, hauled firewood, painted T-shirts, played ultimate Frisbee and dodge ball, and tested the apple launcher David and Sam built for their physics project. Talk about total immersion! Yulong hardly knew what to think of so many siblings in one family, but he seemed to enjoy the ten days he spent with us and has promised to come back again soon.

And that brings us again to December. We have a friend from Great Britain who recently wrote to wish our family a happy Christ-mass. He uses that term deliberately, he says, for although he is an atheist himself, he finds "the Americanism '*Holiday Season*' very annoying in its avoidance of history." Yet Christmas means so much more to us than a historical event! When we celebrate the birth of Jesus, we celebrate the fact that God wrapped Himself in flesh, came to Earth, lived a blameless life, died on the cross, paid the penalty for our sin, and rose from the grave so that we might have life, and have it more abundantly. We pray that your hearts may be filled to overflowing with this life, as well, and that God's richest blessings will be yours in the New Year.

With love from the Flanders family:
Doug and Jennifer, Bethany, David, Samuel, Benjamin, Joseph,
Rebekah, Rachel, Isaac, Daniel, Gabriel, and Abigail Rose

Photo by Nick Neal

2011

Last December was mercifully free of communicable diseases, but cram-packed with caroling parties. The Swiss student who stayed with us during the holidays must've thought that Christmas caroling is The Great American Pastime, given how often we did it while she was here. We caroled for neighbors, caroled for friends' neighbors, caroled for shut-ins, caroled for nursing homes, caroled at the Goodman Museum, and caroled while bell-ringing for the Salvation Army. Most of the folks we serenaded seemed genuinely happy to listen—some even passed around trays of hot cocoa and homemade cookies fresh from the oven—but one old Grinch waved a gun at our group and demanded that we get off his property. I don't know whether his fantasy fudge didn't set or *what*, but he was in no mood to hear "Joy to the World," no matter how sweetly sung, so we breathed a silent prayer for him and hurried to the next house.

January found us checking into a hotel for a week while our kitchen cabinets and floors were being refinished. We slept in Tyler, but took daytrips to Dallas, Shreveport, and Flint for ice-skating, museum hopping, and indoor-waterparking, respectively. This was a great way to ease ourselves into a New Year that would bring many far-reaching and unforeseen changes for our family, the first of which came a few days later when our oldest daughter boarded a plane for Nepal. Bethany (21) spent the next six months on the other side of the globe working with special needs kids. The assignment was all she dreamed it would be and more. When asked on the initial job application to define her expectations, she had written:

I expect to be challenged to grow as I separate myself from a culture that caters to complacency and immerse myself in one that forces me to continuously rely on the

Lord for joy and strength. I expect that it will be out of my comfort zone, and that there will be heat and insects and dirt, but that there will also be love and joy and abundant grace. I expect that God will use this time to continue to mold in me the heart of a servant and to conform me to the image of His Son.... I expect that some days I will wake up and wonder what I was thinking when I signed on for this job, but I know His Spirit will remind me...that "My grace is sufficient for you, for my power is made perfect in weakness." I expect that God will fill my heart to overflowing with love for the people that I will work with, and that I will cry when my term is over.

By February, two of our kids were hobbling around on crutches: Daniel (5) sustained a hairline fracture to his foot, although none of us know how that happened, and David (19) shattered his fibula while bounding down a terraced lawn on campus. He actually heard the

bone crack the instant it happened, but his inertia forced him to take a few more strides before he could stop, which probably compounded the injury. He had a rod surgically inserted that same day, but the break has been exasperatingly slow to heal (fast-forward ten months: November found him in a new cast awaiting a second surgery). Bad news is, he's had to miss out on a full year's worth of ultimate Frisbee and triathlon training. Good news is, this left more time for study, so he aced his classes, completed his dental school applications, and (together with brother Samuel) was named co-recipient of UT Tyler's "Organic Chemistry Student of the Year" award.

We tackled another huge landscaping project in March, expanding flowerbeds, transplanting shrubs, dividing bulbs, adding river rock, spreading mulch, and laying two new flagstone patios. Everybody pitched in to help, including our Chinese friend, Yulong, who stayed with us for spring break, but Benjamin (15) did the lion's share of the work and completed the patios with artful precision. Of course, Jennifer recognized this project for what it was—just one more step toward getting our house ready to put on the market. Doug had been considering a move ever since we read David Platt's *Radical* last year, but Dave Ramsey's *Financial Peace* seminar and Barack Obama's sweeping healthcare reforms cemented his resolve. Knowing this, Jennifer had been praying that if God really wanted us to sell our home, He would just send a buyer to our door—not because she was eager to move, but because she hoped to avoid the hassle of keeping a house show-ready (while simultaneously trying to home school!) or having to vacate the premises at a moment's notice should a prospective buyer wish to see it. So we were only mildly surprised when, without our ever listing it, without so much as a sign in the yard, a colleague of Doug's saw our place for the first time this month and offered to write us a check for it on the spot. We accepted (but didn't close until June).

The rest of the year is somewhat of a blur.

About a hundred friends gathered in our garage on the first of April for a private screening of *Megamind*, followed by a worldview discussion. The movie night was Samuel's idea, and he did a great job moderating: *What part does nature versus nurture play in character development? Does power corrupt or do the corrupt crave power? Are we morally obligated to use our gifts and abilities to benefit society?* Abigail celebrated her first birthday on the 20th. She'd been walking for two months, but would barely say two words. Try as we might to expand her vocabulary, she limited herself to *dee-oh* (which meant "Daniel") and *ee-oh* (which meant everything else). It might've been mutually beneficial for her to spend more time with her nephew Chase, who talked early and walked late, but—alas—Jonathan changed jobs and moved his family to San Antonio back in February…. We signed a 14-month lease on a house in The Woods this month. Ben found it for us, and it meets our needs beautifully. The fact that the owners were willing to rent to a family as large as ours was a miracle in itself. That they let us paint the dining room red and the master bedroom green and gave us freedom to make other changes, as well, was just icing on the cake. In the weeks that followed, we floored the attic, added shelves to sundry closets, sealed the garage floor, laid several pallets of St. Augustine sod, built a wooden fort in the backyard, and installed a flagstone patio in front, surrounded by culls from our Stonegate gardens. Our landlady *loves* us (and the feeling is mutual).

We did the bulk of our moving in May, bolstered by the prayers and support of many dear friends who brought meals, loaned tools and supplies, provided childcare, sent notes of encouragement, and pitched in to help wherever needed. Most of our furnishings fit into the smaller house surprisingly well. What didn't was sold, donated, or left behind. We've been blessed with some wonderful new neighbors, including two homeschooled sisters who've become Rachel and Rebekah's constant companions, but we still miss our old ones, many of whom felt like family after so many years on the same street. Our gregarious Isaac, who has never met a stranger and makes friends everywhere he goes, turned eight this month. It was his "worst birthday ever," due primarily to the fact that we didn't celebrate on the actual day—a *faux pas* almost as unforgiveable as the year Mom baked Bethany a "birthday lasagna" instead of a cake (we were out of sugar at the time… Beth had to fight back tears to blow out the candles).

David headed to Honduras in June for a medical mission trip. He got to clean a lot of teeth while he was there and even did one extraction—great on-the-job training which further confirmed his career choice. Back in the States, he was given the opportunity to do a little cosmetic dentistry this fall. When a freak zip-line accident left 10-year-old Rachel with a fragmented front tooth, Dr. Cannon invited David to help with the repair.... Samuel took the MCAT this month. He did well—especially considering the fact he was only 17 when he took it—but probably not well *enough* to get into Southwestern (Doug's alma mater and Sam's top choice), so he decided to delay applying to medical school and retake the test in January after finishing microbiology and the second semester of physics, both of which weigh heavily on the exam.... David and Samuel both served as short-term missionaries at Joni & Friends this year, a camp for special needs kids and their families. They worked different weeks, but will both tell you that it was the highlight of their summer.

Knowing Jon would be lonely while his wife and sons were in Kentucky visiting Matti's sister, Doug, Ben, and Joe piled into our new Sprinter the first of July for a spur-of-the-moment trip to San Antonio. What is normally a five-hour drive took well over eight, thanks to all the potty-breaks Joseph (13) requested. By the time they reached their destination, Doug knew something was wrong. A quick test with Jon's glucometer the following morning confirmed his suspicions. So while Jon and Ben set out for a day of rock climbing, Doug and Joseph headed to the nearest Children's Hospital where Joe was

MERRY CHRISTMAS

diagnosed with Type 1 diabetes. He's adjusted remarkably well to the four shots a day and countless mental calculations required to manage his blood sugar—I've never seen a child with such tight control. Even so, the remainder of the month was spent shuttling kids back and forth to doctor appointments: Joseph met with his endocrinologist for several hours of continued diabetes education. Gabriel (3) went to the orthopedist after injuring his foot in a bike wreck. He came home with a thigh-high, bent-knee, neon-green cast—a failed attempt to keep him immobilized while it healed (though he *was* permitted to *swim* in the thing, provided we let the cast dry completely between trips to the pool). And Benjamin wound up on a maxillofacial surgeon's table after breaking his nose in an ultimate Frisbee game. The player with whom Ben collided—an ER physician and close family friend—stanched the bleeding before bringing him home, but felt horrible about the accident. Ben, on the other hand, was stoked, because when the surgeon set his nose, he set it straighter than it had been originally: *"That's the best thing that's happened to me all summer!"*

August took us to Legoland in California. Some of our most ardent brickmasters weren't even born (or were too young to remember) the last time we visited, so anticipation was running high. Rachel and Rebekah did most of the packing, and Ben helped plan the itinerary, making sure we allotted time for driving around Del Mar and Beverly Hills to look at the mansions he has long admired on Google maps.

Jennifer arranged for Doug to stop *en route* at Fort Bliss and Kirtland Air Force Base to sign copies of *The Prodigy Project* for the soldiers stationed there. Unfortunately, she came down with a bad case of strep throat the day before we were to leave, so Doug and the kids (Ben on down) drove on without her. She and the baby met them in Tucson a few days later, once the antibiotics had worked their magic. It was Abby's first flight. She did great in the air, but ran her mama ragged during the three-hour layover at DFW. Doug took us to see the Grand Canyon and the Winslow Meteor Crater on our trip home. We ended up spending most of our time in the first-aid stations both places, as Daniel busted his right knee at one stop and his left at the other. *Ouch!*

Rebekah turned twelve in September. Her older siblings all chipped in to buy her a new camera for her special day, which was a surprise so wonderful and so unexpected that it made her cry. She has put the gift to good use as the newly elected historian for the Voices of Faith choir. Joseph had his 14th birthday this month. He's finally drummed up a little dog-walking business in our new neighborhood, having proffered his business card to every dog-owner in our immediate vicinity. If you live nearby and need a responsible teen to care for your four-legged friend, drop Joe a line at *walkmydogs2@gmail.com*…. We got back into the full swing of school this month. Bethany, now home from Nepal, was hired to teach biology labs at TJC this semester (although, like her brother, she had to take a couple of days off for dental school interviews). David and Samuel attend UT Tyler six days a week (including a 7:00 AM ornithology lab every Saturday morning—I don't know if the early bird catches the worm, but he certainly draws the most spectators). The kids at home are still plugging away at their studies, but Gabbers is by far the most enthusiastic about getting up early for school. He loves to learn and is doing his best to keep up with brother Daniel's first grade work. We added a few enrichment activities this fall, including chess club for the little ones, public speaking for the middle ones, guitar lessons for David, Samuel, and Joseph, and varsity basketball for Benjamin. One coach tried to recruit Ben to play football, too, but Mom and Dad think that sport is too risky. "It's more dangerous to be a member of *your family* than to play on *my team*," the man told us. "You've had four fractures this year, and we haven't had any." But he miscalculated. If you throw in the toe Bethany broke last month, we've had *five*.

We went to Big Sandy in October for Family Camp (not quite the same when the whole family's not there) and returned home to find that our big kids missed us every bit as much as we missed them…. Jonathan's family moved back to Tyler this month. He discovered that several of his classes (representing a couple years' work when taken one per semester) wouldn't transfer to the school in San Antonio, so he's decided to finish his degree here. He's back at his old job, and Matti (now expecting Baby #4) is back at her old OB-GYN…. We survived our first Halloween in The Woods. Doug bought ten times the amount of candy he usually gets for the occasion, but we exhausted our supply and had to resort to giving out granola bars, PopTarts, SlimJims and packets of microwave popcorn (each with a gospel tract—see enclosed sample). Even our putting floodlights in the trees and stationing evangelists in our yard didn't scare anyone off. That team of young people shared Jesus with the parents while we passed out treats to the kids, close to a thousand of whom came by before our larder was emptied and we had to call it a night.

Abigail learned how to open our refrigerator in November. Her favorite diversion these days, other than nursing and trying on shoes, is pulling the lids off all our yogurt and using it to finger-paint the floor. The upside is, she also learned to sleep through the night recently, so Mom has more energy for cleaning up those myriad messes she makes by day….

Hot Sausage Balls

Our family loves these, especially the men. I usually make a double batch, thinking I will freeze part to serve later, but they get eaten so fast that I rarely have any left for later.

INGREDIENTS:

1 lb pork sausage (hot and spicy)
2 cups Bisquick
4 cups cheddar cheese, grated
2 Tbsp milk

DIRECTIONS:

Preheat oven to 350 degrees and spray cookie sheets with non-stick spray. Place room-temperature ingredients in a large bowl and mix thoroughly with hands (I wear food-prep gloves for this messy job). Form mixture into 1-inch balls and place on cookie sheet, leaving a little space between. Bake 15 minutes, then turn them over and bake an additional 15, or until golden brown. Serve warm and enjoy!

God blessed us with another pregnancy this month, plus a multitude of friends and family who genuinely rejoiced to hear the announcement, which we immediately sent out via text, Twitter, and Facebook. The sad news that Jennifer soon miscarried was slower to spread, so we ended up having to tell most people in person, even as they congratulated us on #13. The timing wasn't all bad—it just meant we got two hugs for the price of one.... Life took yet another unexpected turn the day before Thanksgiving when our excessively thirsty Daniel tested positive for diabetes. That brings the tally to three children with Type 1, all diagnosed during major holidays. What are the odds? Daniel took the news like a real trooper, although he has since asked, "Mommy? When do I get to *stop* having diabetes?" The answer is that, unless a cure is found, he will have it for the rest of his life. I think it is significant that Daniel's diagnosis came at a time traditionally set aside for counting blessings and giving thanks. It's easy to express gratitude for obvious graces like warm homes, good jobs, sound minds, and full bellies, but Scripture bids us *count it all joy* when we encounter hardships, as well, knowing that our Heavenly Father loves us and can be trusted, even amid tragedy, to work all things together for good. So this year, we are also thanking God for His purpose and plan in allowing into our lives some things we would not have willingly chosen for ourselves—things like diabetes and miscarriage and broken bones. But God is good all the time, and we can see His hand of mercy at work even now. Had our original plans not been derailed, we would never have been in line at Luby's on Thanksgiving Day to venture guesses with complete strangers about how long we'd have to wait to reach the front (answer: 46 minutes). Nor would we have scored a last-minute invitation for our entire family (including Nana and Yulong) to have dinner in the home of some very spontaneous (and very brave!) friends that evening.

So that wraps up another year and another update. As usual, Doug will spend the month of December reading our old Christmas letters aloud to the family, one per night. We love to reminisce in this way—the funny anecdotes trigger all sorts of fond memories, which are in turn relived and discussed at length. The difference is that this year, instead of reading loose-leaf photocopies, he'll be reading from a bona fide book, as Jennifer has now published all our letters to date, together with collected quotes, photos, recipes, and other assorted lists and ideas, in a book entitled *Glad Tidings: The First Twenty-Five Years of Flanders Family Christmas Letters*. If all goes smoothly, we'll follow up with a second volume in 2036. In the meantime, we pray God's richest blessings upon your heart and home this Christmas. Let us hear from you soon!

With love from the Flanders family:
Doug and Jennifer, Bethany, David, Samuel, Benjamin, Joseph,
Rebekah, Rachel, Isaac, Daniel, Gabriel and Abigail

Photo by Janel Merritt

Merry Christmas!

People are like sheep, and Jesus is our shepherd.

"The Lord is my shepherd.
He provides for all my needs."
Psalm 23:1

But none of us wanted to follow the shepherd. We went our own way instead.

"All we, like sheep, have gone astray."
Isaiah 53:6

The path we picked was full of danger.

"There is a way that seems right to us,
but it really just leads to death."
Proverbs 16:25

Soon, we fell into a pit from which there was no way out.

"For everybody sins. We all fall short of the glory of God."
Romans 3:23

We would have died without hope, but the good shepherd came to rescue us.

"For the penalty of sin is death,
but the free gift of God is eternal life in Jesus our Lord."
Romans 6:23

He gave his own life to climb into the pit and carry us back out.

"But God shows His great love for us, in that while we were still sinners, Jesus died for us."
Romans 5:8

All we must do is rest in his arms, knowing that he can keep us safe.

"If you say with your mouth that Jesus is Lord and believe in your heart that God raised Him from the dead, you will be saved."
Romans 10:9

God Rest Ye Merry, Gentlemen
- Author Unknown -

God rest ye merry, gentlemen, let nothing you dismay
Remember, Christ, our Saviour was born on Christmas day
To save us all from Satan's power when we were gone astray
O tidings of comfort and joy, comfort and joy
O tidings of comfort and joy

In Bethlehem, in Israel, this blessed Babe was born
And laid within a manger upon this blessed morn
The which His Mother Mary did nothing take in scorn
O tidings of comfort and joy, comfort and joy
O tidings of comfort and joy

From God our Heavenly Father a blessed Angel came;
And unto certain Shepherds brought tidings of the same:
How that in Bethlehem was born the Son of God by Name.
O tidings of comfort and joy, comfort and joy
O tidings of comfort and joy

"Fear not then," said the Angel, "Let nothing you affright,
This day is born a Saviour of a pure Virgin bright,
To free all those who trust in Him from Satan's power and might."
O tidings of comfort and joy, comfort and joy
O tidings of comfort and joy

The shepherds at those tidings rejoiced much in mind,
And left their flocks a-feeding in tempest, storm and wind:
And went to Bethlehem straightway the Son of God to find.
O tidings of comfort and joy, comfort and joy
O tidings of comfort and joy

And when they came to Bethlehem, where our dear Saviour lay,
They found Him in a manger, where oxen feed on hay;
His Mother Mary kneeling down, unto the Lord did pray.
O tidings of comfort and joy, comfort and joy
O tidings of comfort and joy

Now to the Lord sing praises, all you within this place,
And with true love and brotherhood each other now embrace;
This holy tide of Christmas all other doth deface.
O tidings of comfort and joy, comfort and joy
O tidings of comfort and joy

Conclusion

By now I hope it is obvious that the thing that really makes the Flanders family tick is our faith in the Lord Jesus Christ. It is Jesus who fills our days with joy, our home with love, our life with purpose, and our hearts with peace.

Jesus is also the reason we celebrate Christmas. He is the first and best Christmas gift ever given—God wrapped in flesh, come to earth to pay the penalty for your sins and mine. John 3:16 states it clearly: "For God so loved the world that He gave His only begotten Son, that whosoever believes in Him should not perish, but have everlasting life."

Did you hear that? Full forgiveness and everlasting life offered freely to all. Talk about glad tidings! But, like any other gift, these things won't be yours until you accept them. It is the prayer of our family that if you don't know Jesus already, you will put your faith and trust in Him today, and that He will bless you richly, beyond all you ask or think.

For it is only when Christ reigns in our hearts that we can keep Christmas every day of the year.

More books from Prescott Publishing

==

The Prodigy Project
by Doug Flanders

Love Your Husband/ Love Yourself:
Embracing God's Purpose for Passion in Marriage
by Jennifer Flanders

How to Encourage Your Huaband:
Ideas to Revitalize Your Marriage
by Nancy Campbell

How to Encourage Your Children:
Tools to Help You Build Mighty Warriors for God
by Nancy Campbell

Made in the USA
Charleston, SC
10 December 2011